TOUGHER TIMES
LEANER MEASURES

TOUGHER TIMES LEANER MEASURES

ELIMINATE WASTES IN BUSINESS & LIFESTYLE

DEREK SM OH

PARTRIDGE

Print information available on the last page.

To order additional copies of this book, contact
Toll Free 800 101 2657 (Singapore)
Toll Free 1 800 81 7340 (Malaysia)
orders.singapore@partridgepublishing.com

www.partridgepublishing.com/singapore

Contents

For Christine, my loving wife, friend,
and constant pace-maker that spurs me on to finish this book.

Inspiration & Motivation

The inspiration and motivation I got of putting thoughts to paper of actual manufacturing and service related experiences occurred during my semi-retirement having worked four decades in several Multi-National Corporations around the region. In writing this book, I have unleashed the secrets of Lean philosophies and concepts that were once difficult to grasp but now presented in the simplest form that anyone can pick up and practice without fear.

You may have read numerous books on Lean and manufacturing excellence and could have implemented what you have understood from the those books but I congratulate you to dare read another book, especially this one, as you know very well that other books may not have fully answered your questions. This was what inspired me to write this book in the simplest format that can be easily understood from a simplistic viewpoint of four decades of executing principles and concepts of manufacturing and services excellence.

This book is not meant to add more salt into your wound as you have stumbled on this easy to read version of LEAN and it will not bore you with more 'difficult to understand' philosophies and concepts. This book is just plain simple to read and comprehend and with luck you will be able to implement it with ease.

It is this spirit that you need to catch. Soak and feel the four decades of pains and gains that is laid down for you to unearth and appreciate the various tactics and techniques that had worked by incorporating the salient values of Lean, Kaizen and Six Sigma principles.

This book is intended for anyone who loves a good read, nothing too technical but written at a leisurely pace to enable you to enjoy and associate with the spirit of manufacturing & service excellence and also your work-life.

Pre-amble

This book has dismantled most of the difficult and complex questions often asked while implementing Lean, Kaizen and Six Sigma principles, hence the title "Tougher Times Leaner Measures". It's a befitting time to pick up a book such as this to understand the core principles of eliminating waste and to feel good about it. With the onslaught of uncertainties in the global economy, many people would be caught in this bleak web and will be wondering what else can go terribly wrong with their business and lifestyles. Before anyone can figure out what went wrong, they must first understand the way or trends that have affected their way of doing business and affecting their living styles with more and easier conveniences. Technology have advanced over the decades where conveniences have become user-friendlier and have transformed many lives. It has come to a point where many startups have suddenly sprang up almost daily with ideas and innovations that will blow your mind. The 'thinking out of the box' innovations are so obvious that you practically want to kick yourself for not thinking of it all this while. Lately, most startups appear to be very simple in their approach with minimum processes and investments but the end result of the product or services rendered far exceeds the work put in.

Why do you think this is happening? Don't you realise that lean principles are at work? As we move into the next millennium, you will be experiencing more of such approaches- simple and effective methodologies. When lean concepts and principles were first introduced in the 1950s, books were written by many authors to expound on the real spirit of lean. Alas, the initial publications were more difficult to either read or comprehend as all the terminologies mentioned are not understandable. Only the Japanese were able to catch the spirit of what lean really meant and this caught on just after the Second World War.

This book is less threatening as it is simplified for easy comprehension and understanding as it mingles with light and medium content reading. It gives you a bigger picture of what Lean can do for your own lifestyle and work environment. It is not intended to add on the Lean principles and concepts that are already available in other books but rather it is an attempt to share the background and the techniques to implement them in whatever fashion that you deem fit.

The workaround experiences in finding the most suitable approach to implement Lean is not an overnight thought but rather discovered over trial and error over four decades. This book only focuses on what can and should work rather than give you a very comprehensive proposal which may blow your mind and in the end become more confused and demotivated to move forward.

This book is also written to touch more on the practical applications rather than digressing on the theoretical aspects of Lean principles. The best way is to describe the practical side so that it is easier to comprehend from various industrial experiences.

You can read the chapters in isolation of one another as it caters for a wide spectrum of the understanding and maturity of the subject. Some topics needed additional emphasis and clarity so that you can grasp the understanding and spirit of the subject. It is important that you don't skip these pages if you intend to implement some of these difficult but important principles and concepts.

1

Humble Beginnings of Lean

Lean is not about cutting down activities or processes but rather it's about accomplishing the most value-add results within a given time frame. Every day you may be planning to accomplish a lot of activities, be it useful or not, and go for it regardless of getting the desired outcome or results. You may be familiar with what lean meat or lean diet is all about but when asked about how lean has any connection with your work or your lifestyle- you may or may not draw a blank stare aka: blur. Where is that disconnect? It always appears to mean something that you have to work very hard in-order to achieve lean. It's like losing the fat or excesses around your waist- exercise will take care of that. It is partly true that some effort is needed to ensure that no wastage is created or else the excess will eventually contribute to the non-value add substance called Waste. It is important to note that all the principles and philosophies will not come to anything if you don't have the right attitude and discipline to follow through the various activities that are necessary to sustain the lean condition.

In the early years of huge Japanese corporations, back in the 50's after the Second World War, most of the industries that were destroyed during the war had to start all over again, practically from brown or green field. During this prudent period, the shattered Japanese started thinking through on how to rebuild from nothing except with whatever is left within their reach and that spirit of wanting to rebuild has instilled in their culture to Do Everything Right and not waste anything that can add value to the final result. This has culminated into great companies like Toyota, Nissan, and Honda etc to make their people proud that if they have the will and right attitude to succeed in anything, then, the battle is half won. The spirit that they had was more akin to be a vengeance to prove to the world that they can do it. no matter what the condition is, by focusing on the issues and nothing else.

The rest is history now as the whole world has come to realise the spirit and culture of Lean can be implemented if the people who wants to succeed can also make it. Generations have past but the Lean concepts of not allowing any waste to intrude into their work and lifestyle have stayed alive till this day. Many versions have evolved from the original concept calling it different names as each version varies very slightly from the original spirit of Lean. But by what-ever name you call it- it's still a Waste Elimination process in everything you do.

DAILY ACTIVITIES WITH ELEMENTS OF LEAN PROCESSES

Have you noticed that in the good old days whenever you get to a Postal Office to buy stamps or have your parcel delivered, you would not have to wait in line for too long? But as time passed and as the population and local community grew- you tend to feel that the normal chores or errands have started to take more out of your time. To some it may be quite normal to do that as there are no other means at that time to get such services.

Decades have past and new multi-media technology have crept into our daily lives where letters are not needed anymore as the internet and electronic age have taken over the world- emails or e-letters are written and transmitted at the speed of thought. Smartphones populated the world with innovative apps that allow you to perform real live interaction and communication with anyone, repulsively and instantaneously at the blink of an eye. Nowadays, even parcels can be collected and delivered on your behalf and all you have to do is to click and click your mouse from an array of service providers on the internet. Click and pay for any service and your food, transportation, products are delivered to your door steps. Technology has given you more time to do other things that you did not have before.

Driverless vehicles are already here and very soon- just click your destination and the vehicle will bring you there while you either sip your beverages or read a book and enjoy the stress-free journey through the crowded streets until you reach your desired destination. It can even self-park too. You practically don't need to do anything as the computer takes over your life. What is next in the coming decades- very soon- what you blink is what you get.

Have you ever been into a restaurant and the queue is rather long - wouldn't it be great to just walk into the restaurant and have your drinks and meals served after you have settled into your seats. Now it's possible to book your reservation to a favorite restaurant on-line, pick your menu and inform the restaurant what date and time you will be there. No queues, no hassles and no delays. This will be great if you really do have a tight daily schedule to entertain friends, clients or family and be more efficient to get most things done within the short span of time.

How about waiting for medication after seeing the doctor at the clinic? You are so sick and have wanted to get to bed to knock off your uneasiness but most hospitals or clinics appear to take the 'whole day' to administer the medicine or drugs for your condition. With the rapid transfer of data information between the doctor's room and the dispensary, the pharmacist is informed well ahead of time to prepare the medication even before you arrive at the dispensary counter. Isn't this a welcome moment when you are really sick and wanting to have the medication work on your condition straight away?

Better still, in the near future, all you need is to get a wearable device on your wrist and all your medical condition is monitored daily and you will be alerted of any irregular heart beat or blood pressure condition and these can be transmitted straight to your regular General Practitioner. You will be like a working horse being monitored and conditioned to provide tip top efficiency in your work or life style.

Often times we do have clutter on our work desks and work place. Each day you will be arranging stuff on your table which you hardly use but still you take the time and effort to move them out of the way so that you have space to work. Wouldn't it make more sense to first get rid or place those items that you hardly use into the drawers or shelves so that there is no need to rearrange them on your table every day? You will definitely have more table space to do your work.

Why must there be a need to slot coins into parking meters or scratch out time coupons as if there is a predetermined time to park your motor vehicle? Why create this non value-add activity to bother the driver whenever he or she parks a car. Can't there be a clever way to install meters that only need to register the time when either a smartphone app is flashed over a responder on the meter. And when the owner returns to retrieve the car, he or she swipe the smartphone one more time to complete the time of parking the car. OF course this app will link the payment straight to your bank account as a debit payment.

Wouldn't this eliminate the non-value add activity of putting in coins, retrieving a ticket, getting back to your car, displaying the ticket on the dashboard- and having to worry about the expiry time on the ticket while you are far away doing something else.

Come to think of it- why the ingredients of Chinese food are cut down to size but most European food are chunky. The significant difference in Chinese cooking is that most of the dishes require a quick fry and smaller chopped ingredients get cooked quickly and retain the essential effectiveness of the vitamins and ingredients. And also the chopped ingredients work equally well with chopsticks. Whereas for European dishes the chunky meat need a longer time to cook and have to be cut up by the person who consumes it. It's a toss-up between Chinese and European food preparation- one is the longer process of food preparation and the other is the longer process of cutting up the cooked food before consumption.

Even now with the introduction of faster cars on the roads, drivers are too impatient to wait behind a red light even for one minute- they will either take their chances to zoom across the junction or risk missing an important appointment. Why can't roads leading towards a major junction be lined with sensors that can figure out the flow and congestion of each junction so that the traffic lights are smart in determining the best stoppage and waiting time at each junction? Right now it's only a straightforward timer setting for each junction which really is a waste of time- especially when one junction has no traffic and holds up another that is jam packed. In the not too distant future smarter roads are needed to cater for smarter cars. The ride should be as smooth and as quick as possible to get from point A to point B. More productive work could be done this way and journeys can be better timed for better effectiveness and efficiency.

As the whole world ages, the younger generation will be influencing their lifestyles and perspectives upon people that they meet or work with. They lived through the age of ultra-speed computers, smartphones and mini tablets where everything appears to change with the flick of a finger on a touch screen. There is no need to touch anything physical as it can be done visually and still achieve the same results. In the next few decades, everything will be virtual- and there is no need to use your hands or fingers- just eye movements will do the trick. Micro-chips could possibly be the next wearable devices to manage all of the above accessories- with the blink of the eye and you will be connected to a call, video, smart chat etc. Nothing is more satisfying than to be able to communicate freely with anyone around the world with this kind of technology. If you think this is not possible- then, look back a few thousand years where the cavemen had to make a spark out of striking two pieces of flint- now we can achieve the same with the flick of a lighter switch. It will come sooner or later. Be ready for it.

As for the rest of the activities it's all about eliminating the non-value add processes and still achieve equivalent or better results. For future activities related to work and also lifestyle- the processes involved will continue to be leaner and leaner with improved technology and tooling design. How wonderful it will be to achieve more with less. We have come a long way over the decades to achieve what we currently have. And it never stops- it keeps on moving and changing as if the world depends on it or rather the future generation needs it.

There is always this danger of losing the touch. How did we ever get to this stage of innovation and rapid changes? It appears that products have evolved in their designs to minimize the need to set up anything but can achieve the desired results. For instance, do you have to do much to your smartphone camera to take a photo as compared to a more sophisticated reflex lense camera? Everything appears to revolve around the type of lifestyle of our younger generation where everything has to be quick and done with minimum effort.

Even small children, starting from a toddler to a young kid, their indulgence in computer games, tablets, smartphones, have kept their fingers rather busy on a daily basis. Imagine the day when they become adults, their thirst for such conveniences will definitely escalate. They will not run short of such conveniences as the people who are involved in the design of products and services are also from this generation.

So, the beginning of such evolution must not be forgotten or taken for granted or else this stimulus will fizzle out and die. What we have today is a result of the quest to be leaner in every aspect of our business, products and our lifestyles. Continue to press on and continue to improve every situation and condition and ride through the generations. And it never ends there.

With this end in mind- we shall look back from where we are coming from so that whatever we want to make out of the future and it can be mapped out systematically and effectively. We have to start from somewhere, however little knowledge that we all know with regards to Lean and Change Management, and eventually we shall realise the final situation.

It's precisely the intention and objective of this book that the fundamentals of Lean will be studied and applied to your business and lifestyle in the most simplistic form and it should complement whatever knowledge you already know about this topic. Enjoy the journey as the principles of Lean are unplugged for your reading pleasure.

OPPORTUNITIES OF LEAN- WHERE TO START?

Without making strong references to the principles and concepts of Lean- In simplistic terms we can identify areas of opportunities to implement Lean through the acronym **SLIMWOODS**. We shall spell out each word and then explain what it is all about.

S- represents the **Safety** aspect of your work place or home that creates waste due to man-hour lost due to accidents or minor injuries. In other words the Lost Time Accident (LTA) hours that have been lost as a result of a freak or unforeseen accident at work or at home is considered a time waster on something unplanned and out of the normal work schedule and duties.

It can appear to be something of non-value to you and your family. What if the accident puts you out of action for a few months- how will your company and family cope with your condition? So, alternative stand-ins are needed to fill in your work and your family may need to spend nursing hours to watch your recovery. Isn't all these considered waste? How about your spouse or children- who will care for them, who will drive them to school, their tuition and extra-curricular activities? Who will clean the house, do laundry and cook?

It's unplanned due to ignorance of safety matters at work and at home. Take stock of your surroundings, your vehicles and take immediate corrective measures to prevent them from happening.

L-represents the **Logistics or Transportation** of goods or services rendered that have taken too long to be delivered or presented- either at the work place or on the road. In other words the OTD (On Time Delivery) is unsatisfactory due to delays etc. Looking at the total value stream of the supply chain, each process is dependent on the output of the preceding event. Any interruption in any of the processes will have a succeeding interruption to the input of the forwarding activities. What if the shipment is delayed because the ship could not dock any longer as the docking and loading time has lapsed. The delayed cargo will have to wait for the next available ship to dock at the same port. This may take weeks and if you are unlucky there may not be enough free cargo space left to book the next vessel. This kind of waste may not be so kind to you as the customers may slap a heavy penalty on your delayed shipment. The customer has no choice as he is also slapped with similar penalties by their own customers as well. Eventually it all rolls up as non-value added costs to operations which cannot be recovered from the customers as they have already agreed on the initial purchased price. It may appear to be a tiny amount but it will not only snow-ball into added costs but also create unnecessary work for the succeeding processes. More so if you are transporting perishable items which will deteriorate and dumped as waste.

I-represents the **Inventory** level of the goods produced or the backlog of services either waiting to be processed or delivered to the customers. The scheduling of the materials or preparatory matters are measured by the level of 'out of stock' or 'over-stocked' situations of the WIP (work in Progress) or warehouse inventory level. Additional work was done to store such overstock situation and additional overtime was needed to catch up on understocked situations. Hence wastage of manpower. Additional work means additional costs to the company where it is difficult to pass down this cost to the customers. Why is there always a need to overstock items that you cannot even forecast that will be processed or sold in the short term. These are the hidden areas or blind spots that have obscured every company as this is the easiest thing to do without thinking too much about the consequences of tying up your cash in goods, deterioration of goods, obsolescence if the goods run out of fashion or trends over the months. Worse of all you will need to hire or build warehouse space to manage all the inventory which could run into the millions just sitting there waiting to be converted into sales revenue. It's not the best thing to do if you depend on quick and recurring cash flow to serve other needs of your company. It's not good to have a huge negative cash-flow. Just imagine, your household storage of high inventories of meat, vegetables and other toiletries will give you a rough feel of items overcrowding your home- to the extent of buying another freezer or cabinet to store the items. And this is provided you have space to accommodate these new equipment. Something is wrong here- why live with it when you can have all these tucked away in the shelves of your nearest Megamall? Let them deal with it while you deal with yours. Your house is your home and it's not a warehouse. They should not co-exist as they have different functionalities. IF you think it's a great money saver but when they get mixed, you will pay dearly to the customer for shipping an incomplete component or part and the collateral damage at the customers' side will not only be astronomical but also pose a safety hazard to people who are flying and taking a trip on a big ship oblivious to the dangers they have put them in this grave situation. And if the fault is traced backed to your company as being the source of the incomplete component, then, that's when your nightmare begins.

M-represents the **Movements** of the worker or person performing the actual work or services. A machine operator may be making too much movements like taking a longer walk to retrieve materials, setting the items into the machines and taking further steps more than necessary to complete the job. Here the Industrial Engineers need to focus their attention to reduce the walking distance and apply better ergonomics to ensure the worker zone is just at the edge of the machine zone. Compact layouts and smooth operations measured using Work Factor calculations and simple ergonomic layout will make the worker less tired and become more efficient. Don't be least surprised the worker efficiency may drop as the energy level for the worker sets in and breaks down. Habitual tardiness and absenteeism may follow suit as this is the body's natural shutdown or defense system.

It's great that now you can monitor your movements or number of steps you do take in a day through apps in your smartphone that you can use to monitor and discern on those additional footsteps that were taken to see whether they were necessary or not. It may have helped you clock extra footsteps for your exercise targets but were they of any value to your particular activity? You may be young and also may like it but how about if you are already above the fifties- are you still game for this extra movements?

Efficiency may drop if the non-value add movements are not addressed. Each movement requires a certain amount of calories to be burned and hence the energy generated will drain the body as a whole. Tiredness will set in and distress will also show in the effectiveness of the work achieved. Hence some repetitive activities are currently replaced or complemented with semi or fully automated devices to relieve the worker in this aspect. This will help to reduce and eliminate the risk of accidents to the worker and to the company as a whole. We cannot expect humans to behave like robots as the former is made up of flesh and blood that can only perform well over a limited time frame. Why have the daily work hours been set at eight hours per day? There must have been a study made to determine the threshold time limit of a perfectly normal and able person to perform work most effectively over an eight hour day. But overtime have stretched workers over this threshold and unpredictable events of deterioration of workers' wellness have finally crept in.

W-represents the **Waiting** or Idling time where either the machine is waiting for parts or the last process did not complete on time. This is mostly caused by an imbalance of line processes where some processes are not properly balanced to ensure the cycle time for each process is almost the same so that there is no waste of idling time. Precious working time have been wasted as a result of all these unsynchronized work which has no value-add to the product or service. The waiting is cascaded along the value stream and will interrupt shipments if the goods are perishable items and this will eventually frustrate the customers as their processes will be at a standstill as result of your inefficiencies. It may also affect the incoming items from suppliers and the whole supply chain will come to a halt.

If you are a multi-tasker, then, I don't see a problem in you waiting on your spouse while she shops and you may be digging your face into your smartphone texting to your friend. But in most cases there is always this limit of your patience to wait endlessly. It may get onto your nerves and implode.

O- represents **Over Processes** where the work or services have not been reviewed to cut the excessive processes that duplicates and complicates the work flow resulting in additional work without a proper Standard Operating Procedure and non-standardisation of the specifications of the final product.

Not only is this a waste of resources but also a waste of material and subsequent wasted opportunities of profits as the cost of production has amplified unnecessarily.

This is quite common and often overlooked as if there is no cure to simplify and limit the processes to the core steps which also leads to better results. Sitting back and watch while others do the work may put you in a very comfortable position but this 'feel good' status must be revisited to eliminate unnecessary processes and you will be surprised that the simplified processes may result in higher efficiencies and output. It may be wise to engage or exercise the meticulous detailing of each element of each process to maximize output with the least processes or effort.

A typical over-process situation is having the hotel receptionist requesting you to fill in your particulars over and over again even though they already have the same details in their system (the moment you booked the room either thro' the internet or travel agent). Why generate more work for the customer and also generate more paperwork for themselves? Just imagine yourself getting off a long flight and wanting to hit the pillow in the hotel room for a quick rest. Is this to justify the need for a hotel receptionist? Why not get a credit card reader that can capture all the details as well and all they need to do is to have the customer sign the pre-registered forms digitally on the computer screen? The data is always there- but it's being requested all over again and again wherever you go and it's like a ritual whenever you check into a hotel around the world. Isn't this annoying and a waste of your time to repeat this exercise every time? We must get out of this vicious cycle and look beyond the present into the future of paperless community and society around the world.

O- represents **Over Production** as a result of instable quality levels of the parts or services produced or rendered, respectively. In most cases it is the inexperience of the workers where some appear not to follow the mix of the production schedule and they tend to end up producing something that they feel comfortable irrespective of what the production schedule has planned for the day. There is no production output tracker to prevent this from happening and also the bin or lot sizes of the materials tend to vary and confuses the worker. This is the reason why Kanban methodologies have been developed to produce only when there is a need. As long as there is no signal to produce, then, there is no need to produce. This signal is called Kanban (Visual Signal). In simple terms, take your car fuel meter- the indicator is somewhat like a signal (Kanban) to give you a head start to look out for the next fuel station to fill up and ensure your onward drive do not get into any unexpected 'ran out of gas' situation.

Have you ever been to a fast food outlet where you see heaps of burgers in their kitchen- I don't think so. Most fast food chain cannot afford to stack up or over-produce as the food will get cold and also it's a waste of resource and materials to do so. What they practice here is some form of predictive forecasting and also understanding the eating habits and trends of the customers. This is quite similar to holding a buffet party where you know who is coming, what they like to eat and drink so that everyone will have their fill of favorite food and beverage and nothing is wasted in the end.

D- represents the **Delays** due to a combination of wrong scheduling of materials, machine downtime, machine and worker efficiency and long machine set up time due to wrong sequencing of products that depend on the time taken to set up for each specification. The trick here is to expect delays but not to allow it to happen. Be prepared and prevent it from happening through monitoring of key processes where the few seconds or minutes delayed in each process will cumulate to hours or days of delays. You may have some emergency buffers to take care of this but doing this too often may incur the penalty of allocating non-value add activities and pushing up production costs. Monitor all delays that caused interruptions to the overall value stream or supply chain. Take immediate action before it grows into a huge problem.

Expect delays even while you renovate or build a new home as the total value stream not only involves your contractor but his as well.

S- represents the **Skill**s of the workers or personnel handling the job or process. Due to the misfit of putting the wrong people with the wrong skill sets appear to waste more time than putting in the right core competent workers on the job. Training is one way out but in most cases insufficient lead time is given to train them well before putting them into the job. The easy way of introducing OJT (On the job training) appears to be a lazy or unplanned way of increasing work force for capacity reasons which are mostly in ad-hoc situations where a sudden big order is received for urgent shipment. Not only there is waste in losing some workers as a result of attrition but also the quality of production or the services being compromised. The HR department have to establish a pool of trained workers on standby- usually these standby pool will be trained on Kaizen activities to deal with minute details of the line adjustments or helpers to get certain hick-ups in the processes related to services. In the event of daily attrition or absenteeism these pool of workers will come in handy to keep the work flow moving smoothly and efficiently so that the processes will be continuous.

Most times in any operation or services the waste elements are found in multiple areas and are often interconnected. The iron rule is to complete a Value Stream mapping of the processes and identify the Value-add and Non-Value add items which must be addressed in order to eliminate the waste. The other tool that can be used to identify the root causes of the problems contributing to the wastage and have it fixed at the root so that it does not appear to disrupt the corresponding processes. The Value Stream mapping and the Root Cause Analysis will be dealt with in later chapters of this book. Meanwhile, let's understand the whole picture of where the wastages are currently lurking in the processes waiting to be pulled out like weeds from the grass field and to be chucked off and not to contaminate the good grass again- keeping it to nourish the richness of the earth and grow healthily like what every business process should be doing by pulling out all the wastes by keeping lean.

Building strong Lean principles are like preparing a good ground foundation. If you have aspirations to grow your business and to enrich your lifestyle then you may have to drive the Lean principles deeper so that it will sustain whatever good values are put onto it in the coming years or generations. Why do you think after decades of operations some big corporations are still strong and thriving and why some billionaires appear to have more time for leisure and philanthropy? It's all about sorting out the clutter of their business and lifestyle in the earlier days and are now reaping the richness of the great harvest due to their planting of the good and strong seeds. If they can do it, so can you. Learn from the examples and experiences shared here.

QUESTIONS TO CHALLENGE YOURSELF

1) Do I really need Lean to analyse what is wrong with my work place and my own lifestyle?
2) Do I have the time to do this?
3) What if my team are not up to the mark to assist me to complete all the tasks ahead of us?
4) Will I self-destruct if I just do nothing to help myself and my team to solve the most critical issue that affects our situation?
5) Are we committed and held accountable if we do start the journey of Lean?
6) Why must I repeat the exchange of data and information as if the system have never captured it in the first case? How would you suggest to solve this time wasting activity?

2

Typical Cases of Lean

It is a known fact that Lean was tailored along the same lines of Toyota Production System, aka TPS, and have been modified ever since its inception and application by Toyota Motor Corporation in Japan and around the world. Because of its successes in developing and maintaining processes in the manufacturing industry, the TPS have evolved over the decades to a more flexible principle that can be used across the board in all sectors of the value chain. It has been adopted in almost every field and nooks and corners where it squeezes out all the wastes and adopts the Lean principles to sustain its position and status. The difficulty is in the ever changing landscape of the industry being challenged by newer dynamic forces that were not heard off in the earlier years. Now with the onset of the multimedia boom and the viral power of the internet and transfer of digital information, Lean has become rather archaic if it had not evolved itself away from the original intent of the TPS. Now that it has the flexibility of change to adapt to any change in the landscape it has become more ingrained or have been seamlessly integrated into sub systems of the total supply chain and operational excellence structure where the elements of Lean are embedded deep into the foundations of the newer systems.

Now, Lean is seen to be a complementary sub component of a whole network of other operating systems and management systems which work seamlessly with one another. Especially for the ERP (Enterprise Resource Planning) modules, now you can have parameters from the database to generate Lean KPIs for easy monitoring. This is a shift from the days of past where every bit of current and future state data changes are measured manually. Now you can get it with a press of a button even with nice graphical charts and comparative scenarios of the previous and present state. It is said that Lean has come a long way that it is able to survive the test of time and have stayed long enough to evolve and become a better tool to handle present and future day issues related to modern day requirements of speed and data integrity. A good principle is as good as it gets over time- and definitely Lean is here to stay- in whatever name you want to call it.

Now, Lean is something that is inborne into every aspect of the manufacturing and service industry. But, lately, the Lean principles have encroached or crept into people's lives. Just look at the way how the multi-media world has affected the way all of us do our work or when we take time off to relax. Take Twitter, Whatsapp, WeChat etc- the words and text used have been abbreviated- even words have suddenly become 'leaner'- TTFN, WYSIWYG, WTF, LOL etc. I guess Lean has achieved its purpose and objective here as the user understands exactly what it all means without losing any essence of the meaning of the abbreviation. Similarly this book is trying to do the same as what other Lean Gurus have expounded very well on the principles and understanding of the spirit of Lean. As long as you catch the spirit of Lean, then, this book would have achieved its ultimate purpose and objective.

What has happened is the shortening of processes (example of the lead-times of all the processes where speed and accuracy counts most in the areas of materials and goods transfer)- cutting out the non-value add activities which do more harm to clog the smooth flow of value added activities. Everything can be linked by network like a virtual Kanban system where all the elements move together as one and nothing is left to chance to be wasted and idling with nothing to do. It is so dynamic that the slightest glitch in the supply and value chain network is monitored closely and corrected immediately to keep the chain moving smoothly. But the question is where to start as it takes time to get to where we want to be at the present state. It is by various stages of the implementation of Lean that results can appear and stay improved and changed from the previous state. Everyone knows about Lean but they have not implemented Lean. And why is that? Is it too big a subject to even start anywhere? I believe so because the original principles have been compromised with variations from the true spirit of TPS when it was originally developed by the famous legendary TPS guru, T. Ohno of Toyota Motor Corporation. Different versions of TPS have been renamed as if it was just invented.

LEAN IN LOGISTICS

Now that we know about Lean, how flexible is it when it comes to implementing it to other industries apart from the automotive world? Take for instance the service industry like the delivery companies in the likes of UPS, DHL, TNT etc. What do you think their business is all about? It is definitely about Lean and which element is important in this business? Speed of delivery- the right parcel, the right place and at the right time. So, coming back to SLIMWOODS, practically all the elements are important. Assess the whole value stream and draw out the probable contributors that constitute to the overall issue of the process that affects the smooth harmonious operations. Lean Logistics is all about getting your goods or items from one point to another in the quickest time.

Safety concerns not only the truck drivers, forklift drivers, parcel handlers loading the trucks and unloading into aircrafts but anyone at work or at home- any Lost Time Accident will mean delays for your company, your daily routine and also to the people expecting to meet you or customers expecting to see their goods or project delivered. Someone has to take over the job and most times by a non- regular driver who may create more problems and also slow down work.

Focus on regular training and especially cross training of the group of workers involved in the process. Multi-tasking is necessary to ensure the standby forklift or truck drivers are well versed and follow standard operating procedures. Practise rotation of work and keep the workers motivated and fresh in their minds the various jobs that they do daily or weekly. Keep them on their toes and get them to suggest new ideas or innovation to make their work more interesting and challenging.

Logistics or Transportation depends heavily on the well-kept condition of machinery, trucks, aircrafts and the vicinity of depots, airports and maintenance outlets for trucks to ensure quick repairs and smooth operations of logistic vehicles, which also includes your own car or bike. Anticipation of such trouble can be prepared well ahead by keeping a list of alternative service providers, albeit at a higher cost and also relying on neighbor or friend to pick you up to work. Focusing on a proper set up of periodic maintenance service schedule on all machinery and tools is a must.

Inventory management is also important to ensure all tags are correctly filled and registered in the reception and dispatch systems to ensure real time tracking of the parcels or goods moving around internationally. Without any disruption, the processing premise will not be clogged with unidentified parcels or goods and the practice of First in First Out (FIFO) concepts are strictly followed. A regular and periodic cycle count is needed every week on some high value or highly perishable items must be done to understand the actual condition of FIFO.

Focus on visual controls- like having a yellow box at the receiving area that indicates a time-related process. Any item placed there will be tagged (time log) to be transferred to the next process within the 5 minute window. Some companies install alert signals or flashing alerts for the attention of the worker or supervisor.

Just imagine you do your weekend groceries- you may end up buying items that you still have in your refrigerator- but you still buy it. This is the common mistake we usually do whenever we don't take stock of what we do have and have no idea when you're going to need it- but you still buy it anyways to be on the safe side. It only translates into converting available cash into an item that you don't need now- maybe next few weeks or months. But, why do that repetitively each time you take a trip to the nearest grocery mall? It's rather an impulsive behavior- a 'feel good' that you love to have even if you don't need it now.

Movements of the workers handling the parcels and goods are also an important function to ensure the items are not over the permitted handling weights to safeguard the back and spine. The transfer of goods must be enabled with easy mechanical or automated transfer systems to relief the worker from having to walk excessively and waste too much time outside the processing area where it matters most. Over here the space between processes process

One Piece Flow concepts where the FIFO (First In First Out) is still intact and the sequence of flow of items is in accordance to the promised delivery date. No jumping queue as the plan or other transporters will not be able to turn back and pick up a left-baggage or item which is supposed to be on the truck or plane to the receiver. It has to work like clockwork or else the item will be delayed and the customer at the receiving end will be furious and may opt for another more reliable service provider if you are not able to resolve this hiccup. Focus on semi or fully automated transfers as it will maintain the FIFO and proper sequence based on order and delivery dates. This one piece flow (OPF) concept will ensure each item gets processed thro within seconds and the overall output will also be in seconds. This is contrary to the usual big batch system where there is no respect of FIFO and proper time sequencing- resulting in more delays to customers.

Imagine your own home office or kitchen- do you really keep your items and utensils where they ought to be? Do you ever find what you wanted and it's not always there when you wanted it? Why is this so? Doesn't it take time to open up all the drawers etc to locate and then find it, maybe when you don't need it? But, after finding it, will you be able to locate it again tomorrow? I doubt so. It may be fun to do it once a while but to do it daily will require you to be very fit and agile and also with lots of patience. But when patience run out- you will be back at the stationary store to buy a couple more items which already have in your office or home- sounds familiar?

Waiting time is also another element of mishandling or mis-sequencing the expected arrival of certain items. It could be a quality issue with the items expected to come out of a factory or a printing press or even a dairy farm where the milk delivery did not happen as planned. A shutdown is needed as any jumping queue will affect the process further up and the plane or truck especially the refrigerated trucks to deliver frozen meat cannot wait forever.

Focus on the Value Chain network- getting the suppliers to be strategic partners to your company's vision and mission. If your mission is to

Deliver as Promised, then the supplier must adopt this as their own to realise this mission in totality. Constant feedback and commitment by the supplier to take immediate action and not to repeat the same problems on a daily basis. This continuous improvement or Kaizen is imminent to ensure the workers involved in the work flow understands their responsibility and commitment to the final result of the action or process. Do you ever find it annoying whenever someone says 'wait a second or wait a minute' and it turns out to be half hour or an hour later? Who do you think is idling away precious time? The delayed time is aggravated when the expected time did not happen as promised. It really makes you want to climb up the wall and let out your frustration that someone has hijacked your precious time while they enjoyed every minute of your time doing something that does not add value to your time.

Over-processing also has a role to play especially in the earlier days where multiple forms have to be filled up each time an item needs to be delivered. Now there are the handheld RFID aka Radio Frequency Identification Devices that are linked by wireless transmission straight from the field to the central data processing department of the Logistic company. From that data transmission the whole value chain network is linked and will monitor and push the items across the value chain until it reaches the end customer. This cuts down tons of paperwork and everything goes like clockwork and also seamlessly and it gets tracked across the country and also globally via GPS (Global Positioning Satellites) accurate to within three metres on the map. Focus on the repetitive work of overlap activities of the processes. The Industrial Engineer should be put on the job to understand and pull out the repetitious or duplicative work. In most cases at least 40% of the current process can be shortened or simplified- resulting in lower process time and costs.

Have you ever experienced the processing time in the hospital? The total time taken to process your visit, starting from parking your car, making it to the registration counter to the moment you see the doctor and back to the waiting room for your payment and medication?- the doctor actually saw you for only 3 minutes but the total visit lasted 60 minutes. Why are ID cards made in the first place- why does it ever have to be re-written into another file to suit the computer system etc- which is a complete waste of time and process. Why not have the hospitals scan thro the ID cards (which already have the microchips)- all you need to do is swipe your ID card and the system takes whatever data there is including medical conditions, blood type, allergies etc. All these can be prepared upfront and don't have to be repeated again - wasting the patient's time to fill up another form and waste more time and whatever energy the patient still has left in him (he's supposed to be sick).

Over-production relates to additional work that has to be put in especially for items that are damaged that needed to be replaced, repacked and redelivered and reschedule- adding more cost into the standard work. This is the area where complaints pour in and it acts as a nerve centre to initiate Root Cause Analysis and perform a formal Feedback to the originator or root cause that started this fiasco along the value chain. The better the Root Cause Analysis and the feedback, the better the network flows and the faster the end customer get the products in their hand- safe and sound and as promised to be delivered on time.

Focus on quality of work, have fully trained and certified workers- following strictly to standard operating procedures. Have you ever bought a new or older office or house that have plumbing issues? Leaking pipes and roofs or window seals contribute to rework (repairs)- which are equivalent to fixing a problem which should have been the responsibility of the manufacturer of these items- but it ended up you are the extension of the 'production' line to fix their problem in the first case. It's not so much the money put in to fix the issues but the time and mess that you will need to endure to correct somebody else's problem. It has become a norm in certain industries not to have a responsibility to take care of known and recurring issues. But, in reality, anything that is reworked or repair will never stay fix- as it will come back and haunt you. The right way is to get to the right source of the items that have been tested and proven over time not to create this problem to the customer. Don't create unnecessary waste.

Delays are inevitable but can be avoided. Usually the downtime is related to materials movement rather than data transmission. As long as human errors and equipment breakdowns are happening every day, the delays will be accumulated. But it can be tolerated if the items are not perishables unlike perishable goods, a long delay spells disaster and the countermeasure is always at the processing centre to keep these items under wraps and control and a final check out procedure before it proceeds onwards.

Focus on all types of interruptions- list them out and get to the root of the issues and you will surprised that constant follow-up and getting commitment of the 'troublemaker' to stop this from happening again and again. This has to be drilled into the skull and eventual brain of the worker. Looking from touching on the sensitivities of apathy and sympathy of work stress of the workers-the system must be put in place- usually the culprit is the production scheduler and the overall computerized ERP (Enterprise Resource Planning) hiccups.

Delays in bus and train schedules equally upset your plans for the day. It may not affect your objectives for the day but imagine if it is related to catching a plane or boat ride etc. The additional work to be put in to re-book your next available flight or boat ride takes time and money. Worse still it will stress you out for somebody's mistake. In this case, you may blame the maintenance people for not maintaining a broken down train or boat- but, could it be yourself to blame for not setting the alarm clock or having a late night out and got pissed drunk? Get your life back in order. Unclutter what is non-value add to your life. Stay focused.

Have you ever encountered numerous times already coming into a restaurant and have ordered your food- there was a long wait for it to arrive to your table? Your main aim is to get to a restaurant to get your fill of food as your stomach is at the point of desperation to fuel the energy for your body- but this delay is really getting to your stomach. The pain and groans that your stomach is inflicting upon you is an act of non-value to your body. Your blood pressure and heart beat get pumped up for nothing. There's no free lunch! Would you pay the GST and Service charge after finishing the meal eventually?

Skills of workers at all stations and processes are imminent to get things done right and as per the work standards and time schedules. Proper selection of staff and good raining is key to this issue. An untrained staff will create problems and upset the whole rhythm of the supply and value chain network. Medical attention is also needed to ensure the workers are fit for the job. A worker that call in sick will be either replaced by the supervisor or by another staff from another station who may not have the core competence to do the job right and may even cause problems for the next process and also to the customer. Proper medical aid and benefits are expected to keep the workers healthy and happy. Good living and social conditions are to be balanced with a good working attitude of the workers.

Focus on skill development and certification. The workers need to be recognized and accredited as semi-professionals and not just mere workers. They take pride in their work. Even in the late 70s cinema ushers prefer to be called Seat allocation specialists. They may be right as they know every seat location and very precise to usher you to your seat. And they don't make mistakes or else you have to walk thru the seated knees of other cinema patrons. With all the Lean thinking well thought through for the above elements, I don't see why this logistic business cannot prosper and make huge profits. The end customers will be happy to continue their business with this logistic company as it delivers the items as promised. The art of sustaining the competitive advantage is important and the culture and attitudes of the workers taking charge of the processes must be well taught and propagated down the line.

There is no shortcut to the success of implementing lean as it is a continuous process with constant reminders of what the business is all about- it is the business of delivering value add costs and not non-value add wastes where the customer is not prepared to pay for the latter. The concept has in recent years evolved from a rigid approach to that where it can envelop current issues and suck out the non-value-add activities. In no time that issue will become leaner and easier to get to the root cause of the issue and remain and stay resolved. Get to the root cause fixed and move on to the next issue. Do not give up as long as the momentum, using the right problem solving method, is employed vigorously and consistently pursuing the root cause.

Failures do happen and most people would give up after waiting for too long for results to appear. But they forget that the issues have been developed over many years and waiting for another month or so to get to the root cause is worth pursing and waiting for the results to turn around. In my many years of Lean manufacturing excellence experience on the ground with manufacturers and service providers, it is often said that once you sense a particular issue is the root cause- then if you continue to pursue it until it shows up as true- then you are satisfied after you have nailed it and the results begin to show. It's like the famous detective TV show, Colombo, where in the beginning of the TV show, the first person Inspector Colombo meets, he always hound him or her down as the killer. And he is always right because he had a hunch and after pursing it, he was successful. He was thinking Lean, don't waste Time and Effort. It may be a TV show, but in real life scenarios, it is also true. So, we need that Colombo attitude- hounding and tracking and digging for evidence and data that can assist you to nail the real issues contributing to the waste that clogs up your value chain.

LEAN IN F&B RESTAURANT CHAINS

Why is it that some restaurant outlets at any time of the business day are able to display and serve freshly cooked food items but some outlets do have occasional complaints of tummy upsets; most cases you will not be able to pinpoint the source of the problem. This is where most successful F&B restaurant outlets are thankful to Lean concepts without them knowing that they already made a self-discovery that Lean works. However, if they are not aware of it in the first case then they could have taken years of trial and error to finally discover the lean path. Where do you think the food chain starts- obviously it's the source of fresh produce and freshly cut meat and fresh fish catches that have just been delivered straight from the farm and fishing port, respectively. Also the trust is between the F&B outlets and the known supplier of the items. This is a long relationship that has developed over the years and both sides only focus on the best for the total food supply chain.

Let's study a typical Lean path taken by some sustainable and reputable F&B management teams. First of all the value chain of the source is the root of all problems that end up in the customers' stomach. Obviously the elements to attack and ensure are the following:

Safety of the customer (Food Poisoning). To ensure that the food stuff or raw ingredients that goes into the kuali or frying pan must be safe from pesticides, bacterial infection of meat, fish and vegetables. A known source is needed from the trusted supplier to comfort the F&B procurement officer that they will not cause any problems to their customers. Similarly, types of oil used, beverages etc are thoroughly tested and proven through trial food tasting sessions to confirm what the supplier say. A seal of approval is done to sustain this situation and is confirmed to be the F&B certified supplier.

Focus on bacterial contamination is top priority. The sequence of taking out the meat or fish from the refrigerator needs to be observed carefully. The bacteria is always there to start their mutation the moment the temperature is right. The kitchen hand who helps cut up the fish and meat knows his timing as well and in most times he is the one creating the problem not only for the chef but also for the customer. Never be lazy and work in batches- it has to be dealt with on individual orders even though the next customer has a similar order. It has to be fresh off the pan to the customers' table.

Logistics play the next important part as well especially when certain items are pre-cooked in a central kitchen and then delivered to the various F&B outlets. We do see many tiny trucks, multi-purpose vehicles trucking processed food items to outlets and trucking fresh materials to the central kitchens or the outlets themselves. The vehicles must maintain certain levels of hygiene and temperature control inside the vehicle movers to ensure the food items are kept fresh and clean of any attacks by unwanted bacteria etc. This is also a trial and tested method employed by sub-standard logistic companies but the better and well established F&B companies are smarter to install better equipped vehicles to sustain the freshness of the items. Focus on the temperature controls and the constant maintenance and servicing schedules of all these refrigerated trucks. In the event of a truck breakdown, some emergency generators are needed while waiting for a rescue truck- probably have to wait as the traffic is also another uncontrollable element.

Inventory of raw materials especially perishables (meat, fish, certain vegetables) can deteriorate over time and if these items do not get cooked and turned into dishes on the customers' table, then you are in for a bigtime food poisoning drama and a spoilt reputation and image that will take a long time to recover and gain back the confidence of your loyal customers. Over here FIFO concepts apply strictly as every item has an expiry date no matter how they are ingeniously stored in specially chilled refrigerators etc. As long as the bacteria in those items become active again in the event of a power failure or the refrigerator door was not sealed or closed completely, then you can say goodbye to the items. Timely ordering and delivery of the items plays a key role here. Again trusted value chains need to be established to ensure the items get to the point of preservation, in time, properly processed and stored for the next retrieval by the chef. He must have the confidence that whatever he uses to cook is properly monitored and taken cared off. His job is to ensure the raw materials are properly cooked.

Focus on sampling of frozen meat and fish to take a bacteria count. Don't downgrade them as you will end up a loser if someone has an upset stomach and start throwing a law suit at you and your company for being irresponsible. Weigh the costs and the odds against you and your reputation. Don't take unnecessary risks and don't be penny wise pound foolish. It's not worth it. Believe it!

Movements of raw materials, cooked food and the job sequence that happens in the kitchen also can jeopardise and compromise the freshness of the items and food items. Just imagine the raw materials have arrived at the central kitchen and left there at the receiving area for hours for someone to pick it up and start processing it. Just imagine the millions of bacteria that would have grown over that period. Processed and cooked food that do not get picked up and delivered from the kitchen to the customers' table also pose a problem. It has to be like clockwork. The ring in the bell from the kitchen is like a pacemaker to get the waiter to pick up the cooked items and there is a limit to that- otherwise someone would yell out like an alarm.

Focus on a direct path for processed food- waiters must not be like athletes or gymnasts to maneuver thru the cramped kitchen. Keep the path free and wide open to prevent clashing of kitchen hands and preparation and movements of raw materials into the kitchen. A proper layout is imminent with a sense of continuous flow and the less resistant flow is best- no counter-flows where the meat gets tossed around the kitchen. We often see some restaurants having a showy chef or cook tossing the pan and letting the ingredients flying all over the kitchen so as to impress- actually they are highly disorganized.

Waiting time depends very much on the types of food preparation and the availability of kitchen hand as some items require time to undergo a period of marinating, cleaning, descaling, and hand-picked leaves etc. A good kitchen is to have a controlled stock of readily processed items that are continually refilled like a Kanban process aka Just in Time or prepare as it is being used, if not stop refilling. In this way the items stay fresh and current.

Over-Producing do happen if the waiter wrote a wrong order which the customer did not order. Whatever is cooked may have to be thrown into the trash can as it could not wait too long as the chances of another customer ordering the same stuff in the next ten minutes. Either this dish is thrown away or kept for consumption by the waiters during their breaks. Too much of these mistakes is not value added and the issue has to be addressed to practice a fool proof order taking method as what even famous fast food chains always repeat your orders as they have a quick turnaround time to prepare your fried chicken and Big Mac at the back of the counter- where it's always fresh and hot. Seldom do they make mistakes as their core competence is speed to delivery- you order, the cashier repeats the order, turn their backs, pick up the items, deliver to you within 3 minutes- how cool is that, that's fast food. I call it Lean and Clean. No complaints here except that most times we don't clean up our own rubbish at the table and dispose of the wastes into the readily prepared waste bins. They have a system for us but it's not our culture to follow. Focus is on discipline of staff to follow SOPs and report deviations and non-compliances.

Frequent audits are needed to keep everyone on their toes and each time a new employee is employed and thrown into the job, a mentor-mentee or buddy system be put in place for a short period of time until the new employee get indoctrinated with the work culture.

Over-Processing comes about when standard procedures are not followed as laid out by trial and tested methods. Imagine a bIg Mac being overfilled with onions and pickles that you don't really need. Haven't we seen kids or adults pulling out onions or pickles at their table the moment they got their teeth into the burger. A clever way practiced by some outlets is to ask the customer whether they need it or not- as simple as that. More or less a customized burger. This saves cost to the company but not to the customer- all he got was value that he ever wanted, nothing more and nothing less. Less time and material is used when it is customized- just a few verbal conversation and confirmation and that's it. A satisfied customer who will definitely come back for more.

Focus is similar as described above for Over-Production.

Delays at the table usually hold up the kitchen. And in most times the customer blame the waiter and the chef. Not knowing what you have just done- pondering your nose over the menu and procrastinating on what to eat or order actually holds up the whole process in the kitchen. The materials and the chef is ready but you're not ready. The process just stops and get delayed. That piece of meat and fish needs some time to thaw if you have not given that order. Usually the waiter will take their time before they confirm the order from the customer. This is not good. The focus point is to have the waiter do a promotion- to blabber away the chef's recommendation so that the customer can narrow down their choices rather than scouring their thoughts on the whole menu and still cannot decide what they want to eat. Prompt menu cards laid on the tables or even some posters at the restaurant entrance door could also be a 'top seller'- i.e selling the dish even before the customer grabs hold of the official menu. Even subtle table adverts can play a part to have some customers interested in set meals in which the kitchen can express through the preparation and deliver the food to the table at record times. Normally for office workers who are pressed for time and who don't have qualms taking the chef's recommended set meal do well for the kitchen as they are well prepared to go into action immediately.

LEAN IN MANUFACTURING FACILITIES

The full works of **SLIMWOODS** will be applied here. Since this will be a classic example to bring out the full meaning of Waste Elimination- let's begin:-

Safety: For any manufacturing facility, usually a full time HSE (Health, Safety and Environment officer is employed. The responsibility is three folds-one is for worker and personnel safety, second is company assets protection and the third is to safeguard and protect the Environmental laws of the country. It is a very dedicated and committed job with heavy responsibilities.

Any equipment that gets installed must first be certified accident proof with all the necessary safety guards and bells and whistles to protect the workers and operators using it. Personal Protective Equipment like googles, shields, aprons, gloves and breathing apparatus are usually supplied to workers if they do work in hazardous environment. Regular check-ups are needed if the process involves heavy metals like lead, magnesium etc. Certain types of health hazard materials have already been taken off the supply chain but at times, due to unscrupulous suppliers in developing countries, such materials are still in use. And especially for such materials to be introduced into a third world country where enforcement of banning such materials are lacking, the workers are exposed to long term health damages. Other facilities and supporting equipment and tools will also follow such safety regulations to prevent Lost Time Accidents and mutilation of worker's body parts etc. It is not a pretty sight to have someone's fingers squashed by a thousand ton press machine. There were incidences that workers or machinists have died after the auto drilling machines caught a portion of a machine operator and was killed by the machine. The investigations revealed that all the safety sensors were by-passed by the worker himself to make it easy for himself and also to prevent the machine from stopping in order to produce the parts to beat the daily targets. Such incentive schemes practiced by that company was abolished to prevent another incident like this so that there is no race to over supply to get additional incentives by cheating the safety systems.

Focus on safety is priority and it is always Safety First before anything else. A full time Safety office is needed and a company Safety Committee must comprise a section of all the work areas and be represented in the monthly Safety Meetings. The board must approve the budget with regards to worker and staff safety and to address immediate needs without having to go through too much red tape or tedious approval processes.

Logistics: This area is huge as it covers the transmission of data and movements of materials from the factory to the suppliers and vice versa. In modern day logistics- 3PL aka Third Party Logistics play an important role to support the manufacturing core competencies. Outsourcing appears to solve the most difficult area of manufacturing. However, items put out of sight does not mean out of mind and out of trouble. The value chain is just being shifted from the factory to the suppliers'. Nothing has changed if we look at it in totality. The upside is that the factory don't have to bother with the day to day running of the supply chain management.

With more advanced versions of the ERP system and more sophisticated Procurement and Warehousing Management systems- everything depends on data integrity and data speed from input to processing and output to the next process. With one click of a button all details of the current or real time status of the item moving thru the factory and from the suppliers to the factory can be precisely monitored. The back room boys are the real information technology savvy professionals who will spend every minute monitoring the work flow and data management with clockwork precision. Gone are the days where items get lost in the flow and delay the total process. With such precision it is possible for fast paced production facilities to plan the orders to suppliers in a manner where the items do not have to be sitting at the receiving area but rather go straight to the line side to be used or assembled. This is the Direct Supply principle- however, the competency of the supplier must be to ensure Zero Defects, On Time Delivery and quick turnaround in case there are issues with the supply chain. In most critical processes there are allowances of adding a thirty minute stock buffer on items that require longer lead-times to replenish or to recover. These are specialty parts or materials that come from precision manufacturing facilities or from another nation that may require a day or two to arrive. Some reputable motor manufacturers' assembly lines practice off line ejection of problem parts that stays in the vehicle as if it is still good but tagged for further investigation and eventual replacement or repair offline. In this method, the flow is still continuous so as not to affect 99% of the rest of the one piece flow.

Not so for continuous flow chemical processing facilities- whereby any non-conformance to standards must either be scrapped or reworked immediately. This may warrant a pre-determined shutdown as the process cannot proceed until it is fixed. Hence continuous flow facilities usually are built in modular segments whereby it's easy to replace faulty portions with standby spares or other modules. This concept is called the (SMED) Single Minute Exchange Device without incurring long periods of shutdown. The faulty parts need not be repaired on line but can be autonomously repaired in the workshop while the standby module takes over temporarily. The SMED concept will be covered in later chapters of this book.

Present day warehouse should only take care of longer lead time items and not store up regularly used items which are considered to be fast moving items. The Kanban concept should be employed here as there is also no need to overstock as long as the safety stock level is defined based on the lead time to order an item. Visual controls and close monitoring is needed to ensure the success of Kanban as everything depends on the movements of Kanban cards from the warehouse to the supplier via electronic scanning and transmission of the Bar codes on the Kanban cards. The data received is a virtual order to the supplier to start producing and supply for the next replenishment of the parts.

The storage and retrieval system and bin identification must also be defined. The current practice is not to dedicate the bin space to a particular item but rather to use the system to determine the bin location by the system and the items will be placed in that location for later retrieval when the items are called up by the same entry.

The warehouse must trust the system to do the heavy work of allocating the bin locations and also the physical storage and retrieval by the store hand must be accurate as well. Because human error is still inevitable- some companies have installed fully automated storage and retrieval systems which are fully unmanned and the robotic arms will precisely go thru the motions. A very good and robust supply and value chain network must first be established or else the system will collapse. Toyota Motor went around this issue by buying up at least 15% share in certain key suppliers so as to dictate the cost of production and also the Quality and On Time delivery. Of course all these started with protective attitudes of design and production secrets but now most of these parts are almost sharing the same technology as time evolves. Nothing is secretive anymore as most designs are only different functionally to a very small degree. This is possible as now most Engineers and Designers are not so loyal anymore to stay with one company for life. Times have changed as their thinking have changed and the only way to break out of the cocoon of a fixed working environment or culture. Nowadays independent design houses have mushroomed over the years as they have snatched the talents from all over the automotive world and the cars we see and drive nowadays reflect the ingenuity and talents of these young engineers and designers. There are some portions of the car like the Engine management system may still be designed in-house by major automakers for secrecy reasons and obvious copying by other designers in-order to sustain the competitive advantage. But eventually everyone will catch up with one another. Even now, most cars have similar features like auto reverse parking systems, self-driving systems, special car diagnostic systems etc.

Inventory: Stock of items and finished goods purely depends on the pull system employed in Lean manufacturing. If there is no demand, then there is no production. In this way, there is no waste of resources and processing time. For this reason the pacemakers or one piece flow concepts controls the input, processing and output as if it is one unit of operation. If there is trouble in any area of the chain- then the whole chain stops. It is as simple as that. For most people who don't understand lean concepts- they will say it is such a waste of opportunity to produce parts. But what is the point if the quality is not good or the machines producing the parts are not consistent etc. More scraps or non-conformance parts will be produced for later rework.

Movement or Motion: A most direct flow with minimum obstructions is best. As visualized on top of a mountain when the rain falls- the water will run down the mountain bypassing all obstacles and always find the easiest and straightest path down the mountain. This is similar to Lean. The flow must cut off all the wasteful path and take the simple route with the least resistance. Location of the next process must be as near as possible where U shaped cells have helped solved such problems of having a very long line from one end to the other and having to take a U-turn later in the process to complete the total process. This is not out of design but rather because the factory size do not cater for such long line. It is forced upon the Industrial Engineer to think and devise such U-shaped cells which makes more sense. The U-shaped cells will be covered in later chapters of this book. Overhead conveyor or floor track conveyors are also of help to relief the manual lifting and shifting of heavy items across the process as these are all non-value add activities or can be considered as waste as the customer don't pay for these actions- nothing is changed in the product to warrant a value add that can be transferred to the customer. The total line layout must be as smooth as possible to accommodate such aspirations to have everything transferred on fully automated transfer systems so that the workers can focus on more value add activities like monitoring and inspection of semi-finished and fully finished goods.

Waiting: usually happens when the process cannot carry on unless the resources of manpower, materials, machines and methods are all working in unison. Waiting or idling is a sign of one element waiting for one another to comply before the work can proceed or finish. Of course, everything is expected to move or work like clockwork but things do happen in any of the elements mentioned.

Over-Processing: Continuous improvements are needed to simplify existing processes so that it could be shortened without compromising quality of product or service and the costs saved in doing less will snowball into the profit margins. Encourage Employee Suggestions and implement them as they know better. Anyhow, in real life some of the workers have taken shortcuts from the standard operating procedures (SOP) as they have found a better way to do the job and have increased productivity as a result of his own initiative. What needs to be done is to have those good ideas and practices documented and to revise the existing outdated SOPs. This will prevent a new recruit use expired ones. Be real as the level of competence improves as the workers have spent longer hours performing the processes as compared to the Engineer or supervisor who gave the same old instructions. It's time to change and move forward.

Over-Production: Proper scheduling of products and services is important to respect the First In-First Out (FIFO) principles as it is synonymous with you waiting in line to be served in accordance to the speed of the service at the counter. Why did the schedule change? Is it because materials are not ready? Is there a quality issue? Is the other machine down that could not start up the next variant or type of service? Wouldn't it upset the schedules of logistic trucks waiting outside to deliver goods to the shipyard? I don't think the ship captain will wait for your cargo if the window to deliver the goods to the dock at a certain time frame is violated. The ship has to set sail soon.

Delays related to Idling: Line balancing of work is usually not done correctly. Some newer machines could be producing at a faster rate and some at a slower pace due to age. There must be a proper balance in loading products thru these machines. More so if the processed parts from one machine has to be processed by another.

If the first machine is faster than the second, then the issue of Work-in-Progress (WIP) will increase and create a bottle-neck or traffic jam. All the work done by each machine has a total Cycle Time, CT, which means from retrieval of materials to processing and putting them on racks. Usually racks are just enough for certain lots of production or in batches before they are transferred to the next process. In the event of improper line balancing, there is either too much in WIP or the worker will just remain idle. This is waste of resources, man-power resources, that is. Usually the work station layout also plays an important role to have all processes close to one another without the need for workers to take more than two steps to retrieve or man-handle materials and processes. This saves time in movements enhancing productivity and efficiency of work without tiring the worker.

LEAN IN THE HOUSEHOLD- HANDLING BIGGER CHILDREN IN THE MIDST OF A NEWBORN

The best example of Lean Management in the household can best be described using the scenario of a married couple who have just got a newborn in the home. The preparation for the new arrival appears to be great as everything they have thought of have been prepared well in advance. However, the complication starts as the couple happens to have two other children, age not more than five, who also scramble to attract attention. The dilemma starts when the first and middle child do not appear to fit into the newborn's schedule. No problem- let's analyse the situation and apply the Lean concepts to get to the root cause and how to fix it.

For Safety of the newborn- the baby needs a separate room which is easily assessable by the adults in the home but not the young siblings for fear of disruption of the newborn's sleeping hours etc. House cats or home pet dogs are always a concern and they are best to be caged and placed far away from the newborn. The baby's utensils etc need proper hygiene and kept away from house pets and stashed in a safe location and easily assessable to adults only.

For Logistics consideration- let's focus on where the newborn and mother sleeps. Although they should ideally be in separate rooms but best be in adjoining rooms to limit the need to move too far between rooms especially within the first month of delivering the baby. Resting areas like placing an arm chair next to the baby cot is ideal for breastfeeding periods which may take hours and repeated three or four times daily.

For Inventory consideration- there are occasions for breastfeeding mothers, there may be times the excess milk need to be expressed into feeding bottles. Proper inventory of baby needs require proper itemizing and inventory control to ensure no lapse in available utilities when it is needed.

For Movement consideration- it is best not to move the newborn too much as it will tire the support group (the husband etc). Usually the newborn is on the same level and at adjoining rooms with the parents.

For Waiting and Delay Time consideration- the usual complaints coming from the couple are focused on time constraints- of work, of sleepless nights, of time sharing moments with the other children etc. The root cause is not the newborn but the older siblings. To them, they don't know how all this works and they only know that this baby appears to have taken a lot of time out of the father and mother and the rest of the household. With this 'threatening' feeling, the older siblings will create as much chaos as possible to attract attention of the parents and to draw them away from the baby.

The root cause is in not setting the rules and principles for the older ones to follow and assist the parents to share their undivided attention for all the children. What are those rules and principles? Let's itemize the daily chores and see which processes are key to solving the problem:

1. Most important rule: Both parents and any other helper in the total process of managing the time for the older children and the newborn is to establish a common understanding or game plan so that all parties involved can execute a well-choreographed or coordinated process so that the total flow of the operations is harmonious and don't contract and confuse the other players in the total process.

2. Daily chores- like having a shower, breakfast, lunch, dinner, toilet time and sleep.

a. Time limits for these processes. Similar to every production process to achieve a certain result (product or service)- here the result is to have the child complete the process within a set time.

b. They are not to Over process or Over produce which takes up time and intrude into the time allocated for other processes.

c. Bath time of 15 minutes, Food sessions of 20 minutes and Reading bedtime stories for 5 minutes before bed time are ideal and are limited to ensure the end results are achieved. It's a little bit of time management for everyone to get full attention. And when it is executed regularly with the same discipline, then, the older siblings will get the hang of it and manage their daily chores without bothering the parents- leaving the latter to have time for the baby and for themselves.

d. The daily routine must work like clockwork to fit in the time schedule for all activities- intertwining the processes to handle the older siblings and the newborn- similar to a one-piece-flow (OPF) where every process gets done continuously within the time limit and the end result will be a peaceful and stress-less day.

Of course, you still have the liberty to amend the above to suit the actual conditions. It takes time to allow your older children to adjust to the new arrival in the house and a standard routine will allow them to unlearn and relearn the new family routine. This may also save your marriage.

LEAN IN THE HOSPITALS OR MEDICAL CLINICS- QUEUING TO SEE THE DOCTOR

All of us have one time or another have taken a day off just to attend to some urgent medical ailment and you know for sure the appointment to see the Doctor concerned will easily take up half a day of your working time and you dread having to go through the laborious paperwork from registering your name to paying the bills and still waiting for the medication.

Similar services like renewing your car licences, ID renewals and passport applications etc. They all take up your valuable time-nothing but just to let you wait and wait your turn.

Let's analyse the situation. For all the services mentioned above- they all share the same time-waster elements of repetitive paperwork, non-standard work procedures, disconnected processes etc. Don't everybody have some form of ID where it could be easily scanned and the particulars are all in that tiny chip. Just plug it in and your personal bio-data is splashed across the screen. It takes only 2 seconds to do that. So, don't need to fill in forms that will take up 5 minutes of your time. Next, you will just have a queue number with a pre-determined time to get to the next process with details on the next process- i.e to go to a room marked on the queue chit for your blood pressure, temperature, weight and urine sample – all the necessary data that the doctor needs of you for the current moment. While doing this, the nurse scan your queue chit and it triggers another chit for your next process… it leads you on until the Doctor sees you for a physical check and medicate accordingly.

Just imagine the old way- you fill up a form that will take ages to fill, wait for the nurse to key in the massive data (name, address etc), suddenly your name gets called again after you read the same newspaper at least three times over.

Then, a nurse appear and leads you to the bathroom to have your urine, leads you back to your seat. After a while, she gets back to you and leads you to another room to take your weight, takes you to another room to take your temperature and to another to take your blood pressure etc. Then, you get back to your seat and wait and wait. And finally you get the chance to see the Doctor and he finished his checks and diagnosis in less than 3 minutes. So, what's all this waiting about for a 3 minutes check? You practically took half day off work to do a 3 minute check?? What a waste of your time.

QUESTIONS TO CHALLENGE YOURSELF

1) Have any of the above principles been introduced without realizing that some form of Lean has taken place?

2) Do you find it easy to implement once you know where each parameter has been clarified and where you can carve out the issues and address them?

3) Will it be difficult to implement a harmonious approach if all parties can understand the final results of the various activities?

4) Do I have a say in how other people design their processes so as not to encroach into my time and make me part of a non value-add process?

3

The Lean Tools- What They Are and How They Contribute?

Lean principles don't exactly own any specific Lean Tools but rather these tools were a spillover from some of the tools used by the Toyota Production System. For copyright reasons the tools mentioned outside the confines of Toyota Motor Corporation - most of the tools had been renamed. But in a nutshell they are quite similar with slight variations to suit the changing environment.

So let's begin to name a few and give a short explanation on how they contribute to support Lean in totality.

1) SIMPLE 5S: Whether we like it or not we have to clean up the house with the 5S Concepts. It's quite simple in approach if you can imagine yourself cleaning up your own work place like your working desk. There is a sorting process to get rid of rubbish and things that you don't really need, setting them in order or arranging them in neat corners and out of the way, shining or cleaning the items with dusters or cleaning cloth, standardizing some rules on where each items should be placed each time and finally a Sustaining rule to all users of your work desk- the message is don't mess around.

How can 5S contribute to Lean? It's purely a ritual or habit that instill in you the sense of accountability to your own work place and you are not to get your work place too cluttered with waste or non-value add items. It gives clarity and remains transparent. Anything that violates that space can be spotted easily. It does not take time or effort to spot the non-conformance. It saves time and effort as it is very visual. So, 5S is not only a time saver, but it involves less work, less space requirement and less issues.

2) KANBAN or JUST-IN-TIME: Although this is a famous tool that is easily implemented by visual controls. The word' Kanban' literally means 'Visual Signal'. Most people use the Kanban Card as a signal to indicate there is a need to fill fulfill an order for this item and it triggers the supplier or the previous process to send the refills of materials or sub-finished products. In other words the process is quite simply confined to signaling the previous and forwarding process of the current status of the work in progress and the raw materials condition. With the generation of new orders in the form of Kanban cards, the process self-automate itself and it moves like clockwork. Of course the movements and scheduling of the Kanban cards are perfectly timed based on the lead time of each process and lead time of suppliers etc.

How can Kanban contribute to Lean? Kanban eliminates the need of more space for excess WIP; eliminates waiting and idling time; contains defects if they ever happen; faster cycle time and ability to coincide with the tact time. The tact time is like the pulse of the whole factory where it is determined by dividing the available working time over the total monthly orders. As long as the cycle time of each process is in synch with the tact time, then the condition is a constant and continuous flow. This condition will eliminate batch flows and encourages one piece flow capabilities which eliminates excessive material handling and transfer times. The finished goods will be completed within the tact time and in the sequence of sales promised dates.

3) ONE PIECE FLOW, OPF: To elaborate further let's take an example of two scenarios:

Scenario 1: A product needs to go through four stamping processes. This factory has set up four types of metal presses with different tonnages. Four operators are manning the four presses to prepare the steel plates with oil and input the plates into the individual presses to be stamped and later removed and dumped into baskets. The baskets can contain at least fifty pieces of the stamped parts and are conveyed to the next press station to be processed. Eventually the items get thru the series of four press works.

Scenario 2: Similar situation as the above factory but this time the four presses are linked with electro-mechanical transfer mechanisms that link the four press dies. The mechanism is mechanized to pick the steel plates to load into the press dies. Simultaneously the mechanism does that for the four press works and work in tandem in one coordinated movement, loading, unloading from each process and moving the press works from the first to the last press and finally dropped into a basket. The difference of the two scenarios is obviously very distinct. Scenario 1 has to employ four operators as compared to only one for Scenario 2 which only has to employ one operator to watch over the electro mechanical mechanism. The other observation is that Scenario 1 uses the batch system building up small batches of units in each station and transferring them along to the next press and so on which involves idling time of the presses when they do that.

Scenario 2 practises one piece flow (OPF) where the sheet metal is loaded by mechanisms and transferred simultaneously until the last operation without the intervention or stoppage of the presses. The machine or press time is fully utilized.

In modern factories that are geared for high volume press works- the sheet metals come in roll form where the sheet metal is pulled thru the series of press dies that are lined to cater for smooth transfers.

How can OPF contribute to Lean? Obviously it reduces the need to man-handle the parts; the machine keeps running and pressing the parts; it is safe for the worker; the skills of the worker need not be too high as they only need to watch over the mechanism to work well; better throughput of parts and able to beat the tact time; better quality of parts; no in-process WIP, can meet the promised leadtimes as the process is in sequence of the order dates.

This is akin to passing a pail of water with a long line of helpers where the work needed for each helper is to pass the pail from one person to another without even having to take a step and not even having to place the pail into another cart or trolley but just swinging the pail of water and passing it on. The OPF is similar to this methodology and it has been practiced without you even thinking about it.

4) TOTAL PREVENTATIVE MAINTENANCE, TPM: This is an important part of the factory operations. It involves the full management of all the scheduled repairs and services planned in accordance of the duty cycles or operating cycles of the machines and the special tool and dies. The OEE or Operational Equipment Efficiency index must attain at least 92% to ensure there are no unplanned shutdown of machinery. The OEE is calculated by multiplying the Rejection Rate, Uptime Rate and Machine Efficiency. For world class TPM the OEE is around 96%. TPM is divided into two sections. The first being the normal Scheduled Servicing and the second is the unplanned but autonomous repair capability. The normal service is straight forward as the shutdown of the machine can be pre-determined. However, the unplanned autonomous repairs could be due to some worker making a mistake and damaging some portion of the tooling etc. In anticipation of such unplanned breakdown, the tooling are normally snapped on where it can be removed within a minute and a stand by unit is snapped on within a minute as well. Here we can define such repairs or set ups as SMED (Single Minute Exchange Devices). Every minute counts in a fast paced production line. The autonomous concept is able to eject the defective tooling out of the machine and repaired in the machine shop while the machine still continues production with a standby unit.

How can TPM contribute to Lean? It increases thro put by cutting down waiting and idling time. Efficiency of tooling and machinery is good and stable resulting in better quality products all the time, pre-determined inventory of spares that are always ready and available as planned and set up time can be predicted.

5) ZERO DEFECT CONCEPT: This concept predetermines the level of defects based on the Total Cost of Quality. This includes the cost of rework, warranty claims, logistics and other travelling costs of personnel to repair on site and parts replacement costs. A budget is set to ensure the actuals do not go beyond the predetermined figure. Based on this target, every section will control the production and recovery costs and are reported weekly to the finance department to make the necessary calculations on the Total Cost of Quality of the total parts produced for that month. Any deviation from the predetermined value can be easily detected.

How can Zero Defect contribute to Lean? No extra space is created to accommodate inefficiencies, no additional hours spent on repairs and recovery, no substandard repair quality, reduces delays and need of re-scheduling more parts to replace and recover the deliveries. Overall the cost control will improve the profit margin. Most companies have the wrong notion of Zero Defects and are only interested in the outgoing quality levels of their products. But if you consider the repaired unit as not having a defect on its way to the customer, then you're wrong. The customer is the last process to determine whether your product is up to standard or not. For this reason all processes must be accountable for everything- it's like a factory within a factory in each process where there is an in-bound of materials, go thru some form of work and then the out-bound process of transferring to the next station. The inbound, WIP and outbound are the responsibility of that station to ensure the specification is correct, the add-ons are correct and the quality is within limits. By monitoring each station as if it is a factory I believe the Zero Defect concept will work thru out the total factory till the product reaches the end user.

6) POKAYOKE: This is a Japanese word for built-in fool-proofing where the workers can never make mistakes. For instance if we have two parts to combine before processing them- there must be indicators or certain shapes in both parts that they will match before they can be put together. Automation has advanced over the years where tiny video cams are attached to tooling mechanisms that can recognize the orientation and shape of the parts to be assembled. The video does a micro second recognition and alerts the machine to stop if the parts used are incorrect. These types of Pokayoke devices are widely used in fast moving electronic industries where a few hundred tiny components are assembled together at very high speeds.

Simple Pokayoke examples like the assembling of symmetrical parts but with a slight difference in one of the symmetrical halves. Most issues come from assembling two halves that are exactly identical but is a defect. It should be one that appears to have another hole and the other should not have one. For such cases, usually a pokayoke jig is needed to first have the half with the hole set on the jig. The pin will allow the setting for the half that has a hole but will not set the part that has no hole. This simple fixture is enough to ensure 100% success rate that there are no slipups.

Ever had a problem identifying a jar of material and not sure whether it is salt or fine sugar. The sure way is to taste both and decide. Ever wondered why the pepper and salt dispensers have different number of holes for dispensing. Is it still fool proof? The way out to ensure salt, sugar or flavor essence are correctly stored and used is to put them in containers that are completely of different shapes. As these three similar colored and similar textured condiments always get you confused at home, then it's time to take some action. Purchase three dispensers of odd shapes and make sure they are of clear glass. The sizes should differ the one for sugar is the largest followed by the one for salt and then the taste enhancer. The dispensing spouts should also be different. The one for sugar must have a longer spout, followed by a short one for the salt and a flat cap (with some tiny holes) for the taste enhancer. For better recognition labelling is also encouraged.

How can Pokayoke contribute to Lean? No mistakes, No rework needed, quality is assured, production efficiency is high, no delays and lead time of delivery is predictable. Installation of electronic bells and whistles will guarantee an absolute 100% ideal process.

As for the kitchen, the tongue of the chef is the human 'bell and whistle'.

7) **SMED:** The Single Minute Exchange Device is synonymous with a Quick Snap On devise that facilitates a quick release and lock of a tool die, sub equipment or a consumable item like a cutting blade, grinding

stone or jet nozzle. The idea is to enable the TPM personnel to eject the defective tooling from the machine in within seconds where he will simultaneously exchange it with another standby unit and get the machine running again. Then the defective part will be handled off line in the machine shop.

To facilitate this for all the machines- the SMED mechanisms must be designed into each equipment throughout the factory. Even for huge stamping dies- transfer tables lay beside the one that is operating. Once the working die is scheduled to be taken off the press, the existing one will be disengaged by releasing the Snap On devices and the standby unit will snap on and the press is ready to go. In very efficient press shops, all the die changes occur within single minutes of stopping the press.

Formula One racing is a perfect example of a car having a pit stop for 11 seconds where the four tyres are changed and the fuel is filled to the brim and off it goes. It's all about quick release locks for the tyres and a high pressure fuelling hose. And if the driver need to go for a pee, the steering wheel snaps open with a push of a button and off he goes. In most steamboat restaurants, mini gas cookers are used. They have stopped using pipe-in gas lines and also stopped using 12 or 15 kg gas canisters and opted for the miniature gas pellet canisters that can easily snap in and out very quickly.

In the audio-visual industry, SMED is also applied here. In the old days records are played on turntables until the cassettes revolutionised the music world and now we have ipods and wireless music from the web.

How can SMED contribute to Lean? Optimisation of capacity, no idling and waiting time, allow more time for autonomous repairs and services of tooling resulting in better quality tooling, savings in spares for unexpected breakdowns, predictable TPM scheduling and cost control.

QUESTIONS TO CHALLENGE YOURSELF

1) Have you thought of which area to intervene and explore further to implement Lean?

2) Are you confident that it can succeed given the tools that were briefly explained to you?

3) Depending on which issue you are facing, isn't it a good practice to do first things first, 5S, VSM and Problem Solving to identify the priorities?

4) What will it take in terms of competency to get your team members to understand the Lean tools?

5) Have you got a plan to train them externally as you do agree that these tools are helpful?

4

First Things First- Unclutter Everything Before adopting 5S

Not until the late 80's that 5S came into the scene. This was the buzzword in everyone's lips as if when you mention this word it is like magic and everything appears to be okay. How they have wished that it was so easily implemented. 5S appears to be the principles of a culture that does not come over night. It took generations from the days of the Samurais and Ninjas and also from the Imperial Courts that this culture has stayed as it was back then. As years passed, many businesses or management teams have ignored the basic principles of it being a sustainable program that is usually a part of and the key component of establishing a visual workplace and are both a part of Kaizen- a system of continuous improvement- which is a component of Lean. But over the years with the repetitive exposure of working people to Japan and Taiwan, they have noticed that 5S have sustained and thrived and it has enriched the lifestyle of these people who are always disciplined and orderly in their everyday lifestyle and mannerism.

Fortunately, it didn't fade off over the decades as it is making a come back and catching on strong in newer corporations and international businesses as they have seen the benefits of big corporations which sustained 5S and prospered. Good things never seem to disappear, they just fade in and out- they are the main fundamentals that form the pillar of any new or existing corporation and this augers well for building new initiatives over very strong fundamentals. It requires the whole organization to adopt the principles so that the culture will sustain for generations to come.

WHAT IS 5S?

Its an acronym to represent the following Japanese principles:

Seiri: Tidiness

Seiton: Orderliness

Seiso: Cleanliness

Seiketsu: Standardisation

Shitsuke: Discipline

Or in layman terms:

Sort, Set in order, Shine, Standardise, Sustain. Simple to understand and remember vaguely. To understand the above principles clearly, let's assume you do have a work desk at the office or at home. What do you do whenever you sit down at your desk? Yes, shifting things around like computer mouse, stray usb wires, sheets of paper, calculator, books etc. What exactly have you just done- you're right, shifting things which you dont need at that moment- just trying to create space on the table so that you can start doing some work on the desk. Isn't this considered a wasted activity?

What if you use the 5S principles? First of all Tidy up your desk- ie remove scraps and things that you don't really need now; create some orderliness by putting the books back in the shelf, keeping calculators in the drawer, purchase an organizer to keep the pens, pencils and clips; Clean up the desk. You have just exercised the first 3S and you are almost done. The 4S and 5S principles are more for sustaining the new state of the condition of your desk be it at your office or at home. Standardisation is required as it will maintain the 3S and Discipline has to be driven into your daily habit to ensure the standardization stays that way. Isn't this simple?

You may think- if it is that simple, then, why 5S appears not to be the first thing that anyone or any company should do? The reason can be easily explained that it takes the top management or the company leader or head of the house to practice 5S. In Japan it started from the highest institution- the Imperial Court. It cascades down to the simple commoner in the farmland. IF you take a trip to any of the countryside of Japan- you can see real life 5S practices that the people practicing it appears to do it as if it is their life and frankly their life depends on it. We do know that Japanese homes are rather small in size and it cannot contain all the luxurious items that are available in the market. It is not strange that in the 60's and 70's the electronic and house hold appliances appear to be designed to suit small condominiums and small houses in Japan. Everything appear to me mini in size. Lean is practiced here where space is a constraint and the products are downsized to optimize on the available spaces.

And 5S is important to get rid of unwanted stuff and only keep essentials in the home. So, 5S has become a way of life for the Japanese. Are you ready to adopt this culture and habit in your own home and office or company? How ready are your workers and staff? Are they ready to unclutter everything and stick to these principles to have more clarity?

Even in olden day China- we have this Spring cleaning period especially as it signifies the end of Winter and every household will start to sort out the broken roof due to the weight of the snow and mending broken wells as the ice that developed in winter have penetrated and torn apart the wall cracks. It was done for centuries as if it is part of their culture. Today we only know it as Chinese New Year where the Chinese fondly call it Spring Festival. It's a joyous occasion to sweep away bad luck, bad omens with the firing of crackers to scare away unwanted spirits etc. In modern times it has lost part of its meaning as the economy have improved and farmers are not considered poor any more as they have huge bungalows and good machinery to take care of all their ancestor's woes. But, reality has taken one full circle and most companies and homes have re-cultivated the practice of 5S- especially so during the 2008 Summer Olympics in Beijing where the whole city was transformed and homes were spruced up with repairs and fresh coat of paint as the whole world will be watching Beijing and the influx of visitors from overseas who have not been to China and first impressions matter. Of course these actions are good but not on ad hoc basis; best to have it done and improved all the time.

5S IN MANUFACTURING FACILITIES

As mentioned earlier the Lean elements were more focused on manufacturing environment as the scope is very large. However, there is no limitation to what 5S can do for non-manufacturing concerns which covers the service sectors as well. All good things developed for the manufacturing sector has maintained a certain level of sustainability to most businesses.

All newer designs for green field manufacturing facilities have the hallmarks of a lean and clean layout. The 5S principles are more or less built-in where machines are properly grouped and the material access and flow is smooth and free of obstruction. Every inch of the shop floor is optimized for better efficiency of movements of materials and people. The 3S portion is easily handled by automated equipment, tooling and overhead conveyor systems and the remaining 4S and 5S is dependent on strict process documentation, training and sense of responsibility and commitment. Some companies especially in the electronics environment- 5S competitions are set up and each month the wining section or line will be rewarded with small gifts as an appreciation of their participation and commitment to ensure the 5S level is maintained. This kind of friendly competition is encouraged so that the rest of the factory will be excited to participate and commit their time as well to 5S. It is not always necessary to have such teams working separately outside normal working hours to keep and maintain 5S at the workplace. The emphasis or focus is to imbue into each worker of the company to take full accountability of 5S and be committed to it for their self-development and becomes their habit. As years past, whatever habits practiced in the company will eventually cascade into the lives of the workers and that is where the culture begins to evolve as they embrace this habit daily.

PRACTICAL PLAN TO IMPLEMENT 5S

This is often neglected whenever a company or individual have decided to start 5S. In their mind they only can equate to 5S as cleanliness and having items lined up in orderly manner etc. But having known the real principles of 5S which is a sub component of Kaizen and Lean – then the whole perspective opens up. The present state of 5S in your work place may be already existing for some time and the people may have grown to be happy of what they have got and since nobody is unhappy of the current state of 5S then no further work or effort need to be done. But, we know this is wrong.

First thing to do is make an audit of the current state of 5S. The top management should appoint a 5S facilitator or Officer to be fully in charged and accountable for whatever activities are to be prepared and implemented. A simplified 5S check sheet is sufficient. The following steps are strictly followed:-

1. PREPARATION: Form a 5S committee comprising of at least 2 members from each section across the whole company including office staff and also people from outsourced service providers (waste disposal, materials despatch etc), you will be surprised that a large portion of the 5S woes come from these areas, there is an old saying- out of sight and out of mind. The members are the motivators or facilitators to implement and follow the guidelines to achieve weekly, monthly and yearly targets. Each particular section may have different rules and conditions to keep the 5S intact and in order due to the nature of the process, equipment and hazards involved.

Draw out the 5S zones and place the lead representative to be accountable for their defined zone. They are to safeguard their zone from within and outside the zone. Anyone within the zone violates the 5S principles will be 'punished' i.e cleanup for everyone for a week etc and anyone from outside this zone will be penalized- minus audit points if the other zone have violated theirs. Everyone responsible for their own 5S zone will eventually safeguard their zones with their dear lives. This is like a war zone but it works!

2. 5S Audit Worksheet: This is a simple checksheet in which you can develop on your own depending on the type of business you are in:

1S: SORT. What does the first 5S principle say? Sort out the items that clutter your daily work or interferes with your flow of work. Its like a big white elephant in the room, no one seems to care even if they see something big but as long as they can maneuver around its okay. But, it violates the 5S principles- so get rid of it. But, be careful here as the committee needs to know and approve the disposal of company assets that have yet to fully amortised its value. This decision must first be fact checked and the finance manager to sign off the item that have been singled out from the clutter to be disposed of.

3. RED TAGS: The Finance dept will assist these Red Tags- identifying the item, location of item, why it was identified to be disposed, what is book value and Final decision to Stay, Store or Scrap. If approved, move them out of the job site.

4. 2S: SET IN ORDER. At the end of the week or month, after the identification and removal or disposal of the unwanted items from that particular work place, there will be spots of free space and better clarity of the total work place which was never seen before. This is the golden opportunity to get the Industrial Engineer to revisit this area and think hard on how to unravel the mistakes done by his predecessor on a bad layout and now has the opportunity to make it right. As a result more free space is recovered as the remaining equipment, racks, tooling racks go thru makeover in the layout. Suddenly 5S has given back the company free available space for free to put in better equipment to increase productivity and upgrade the quality of the products. Isn't this amazing in not having to put in investment to extend the existing premises to accommodate a capacity increase. Just imagine the amount of free space that the company can recover or reclaim if every section follow just the **1S**

As the sorting exercise of 1 S proceed over the months, the Facilities and Engineering sections must work with the Production department to determine the work flow and processes that they need to shorten or refine. The final result will determine the outlook of the new factory layout. This will not incur massive investments as the equipment and other supporting items are usually portable. What is needed is to re-align and reinstall air, water, gas and other facilities to support the new location of the existing and new equipment. These costs are drawn from the maintenance budget and do not need approvals for capital expenses.

This is the opportunity to make the layout compact to minimize movements of workers and also materials which are all elements of Lean to reduce movements of workers, walking distances and also cut short transfer and waiting time of material transfers. The 2 S in-fact restructures to build in Lean or eliminate wastes. So now your perception of 5S has suddenly awaken your thoughts- 2 S is a Cost Saver and Waste Eliminator. But, its not finished yet! There are better things to consider. As we all know already, everything is dynamic and the current state is always changing as the situation in the factory changes in accordance to the market forces. For this reason, lines are drawn to keep every item in place. If you have ever gone into a full 5S factory environment, the factory floor has defined walk ways, production areas, machine zone, materials zone and worker zones. Everything has its place and are all set in order. By doing so with colors- walk way (usually green); production are (light grey); Materials (blue); Equipment (bright orange) and equipment color (mostly light apple green or navy blue with bright yellow on safety features). This visual display is part of Lean as everything must have its proper recognition and place. And all these visuals require a great respect to be maintained so that any non-conformance can be easily recognized and put back or set in order again. This Lean technique eliminates time loss during a peak period of the process as it focuses on compactness of the layout and the motions needed to finish the job in the least number of steps.

1. SCRAPS AND REJECTS? We have mentioned that the outsourced agents who come in to collect scraps from the factory also be part of the overall 5 S committee. Rules of storing and retrieving scraps must be strictly followed. The scrap bins must have certain dimensions and color coded to contain paper wastes, scrap steel, heavy metals, lubricants and hazardous substances. Proper identification and protection must be followed as per the Environment, Health and Safety regulations of the land. Periodic disposal of such wastes and scraps re regulated in accordance with the speed of production. The more the products are produced, the more waste is produced.

The rejects are usually reworked or recycled and such space is needed to organize the work flow so as not to contaminate the flow proper. It is usually designed as a staging area and limited to a small lot. Anything bigger like an overflow of rejects will trigger an alarm to stop the non-conforming process and fix the problem. A Root Cause Analysis must be done to ensure no rejects surpass a certain percentage of production which is usually monitored and determined by the quality department.

2. 3S: SHINE. The equipment or items that are retained may need to be serviced and given a new coat of paint. The color scheme must follow the industrial norm as mentioned earlier. The colors will spruce up the working environment and gives it a more pleasant surroundings. Colors can and do put the workers in a better state of mind and eventually work more efficiently with less energy and effort. Everything is supposed to be where they should be, easy to retrieve and kept and easy to spot non-compliances and also easy to make reports to the relevant teams or persons responsible. Even a spec of oil or strayed rubbish on the production floor is noticeable. Equipment that has many safety sensors are usually spray painted or zone off with bright orange colors as it's a standard global color for safety. As we remember carelessness of workers usually lead to Lost Time Accidents which is an element of Lean where there is waste of worker resources if-ever they get hurt while working and have to be either admitted in hospitals or stay home to nurse a nasty injury. But still the company pays his salary but someone else need to take over the job that is left unattended. All equipment and material racks must maintain their condition. Teams will need to regularly touch up slight damages to the paint surfaces of machines, racks and even the worn out floor lines so that the 5S principles continue as if it is part of the working culture and habits.

The machine and material zones need to be respected by the worker as he has to stay within his production area. Usually it has to be a few steps (usually not more than three steps) for a worker to reach out to get materials to load into or remove a processed part. Each zone must be respected so that every layout will follow the same pattern. However, since Kaizen or Continuous Improvement is practiced in support of Lean, all feedback from the workers, facilities technician, material handlers and safety officer are reviewed with the Industrial Engineering department to make changes and continue to improve the flow and efficiency of the work.

3. 4S: STANDARDISE. Depending on the size of the manufacturing facility. Having the existing committee to control all the principles of 5 S may be a huge task or a big ask. As and when the 5S culture sets in eventually, everything that is required to be followed and maintained must come from standard operating procedures, SOP. All aspects of 5 S, Kaizen contributing to Lean ideals must be spelt out in terms of 5 S posters, 5 S Principles coupled with regular training of leaders and facilitators. Certified 5 S leaders must ensure new recruits go thro the 5 S induction together with the HR and Safety officer so that the new recruits have a mentor watching over their shoulders on this important discipline. All color schemes and types of machines, racking designs and work standards must be carefully coded and registered so that any new layout or machinery purchase follows the color codes, size of machines and safety features. Special machines will also not be spared as eventually they are subjected to the same rules. Only the 5 S committee chairman is allowed to deviate special cases.

Standardisation of periodic TPM or Total Productive Maintenance of machines and other supporting items in production also play a key role to ensure smooth flow of products throughout the factory. TPM can predetermine the shutdown of certain machines without interrupting the production schedules. This is the term called Autonomous TPM where most fabrication dies are designed for Quick Release and Replacement which is also a feature that supports Lean in not having to stop the machine for over a minute. SMED or Single minute Exchange Devices is common in electronics and plastic injection facilities where every minute lost represents a few hundred or thousands of product throughput. This is where every minute counts. The TPM team will have in their arsenal the standby components to set up for the next range of products or to intercept the production tool that has reached its duty cycle and has to be replaced.

4. 5S: SUSTAIN. The best part of walking into any factory environment is anytime of the day and night- the 5 S condition is sustained like clockwork- no one to watch over the workers to ensure they follow the rules etc. How is this possible in some industries? It is not because they have installed more CCTVs to watch over them- infact it is the other way, the workers are watching the other zones on how they perform during the weekly 5 S audits. Yes, they have come to a matured state of self-auditing their own zones as it represents their pride and commitment for themselves. They have kept their zones in 5S condition for themselves and not anyone else.

They use to say "you must be able to eat off the floor". Not recommended to be adopted by restaurants but that saying says a lot. It reflects the culture of the people running the manufacturing environment. Even the toilets are spick and span with the aroma to make you feel like you are in heaven. Toilets are a place to relax and rest- not one to pinch your nose and hurt yourself falling off a slippery floor or cut yourself on a broken mirror etc.

Sustaining 5S is the ultimate goal of every operations as it represents a model or benchmark and projects a respectable image which also transcends into the product as a good quality product produced by a cultured and united team of workers who take pride in their own environment and high level of commitment. Duplication of the sustained state must be of the current status. Any improvement made at any time must be cascaded to all areas of similar processes or any items that can improve the current state. This change is continuous as the Kaizen mode is always in real time and the benefits it reap to support Lean will be seen in the bottom line of the business.

Most companies have seriously set up 5 S offices to promote it to a very serious level of competition amongst different areas of the same factory and also amongst different factories of the same group of companies. Self-audit is one thing that is local but cross audit between different auditors have also started and worked well to keep everyone on their toes and to cancel out biased audit practices. All in all it is for the best for the company as a whole as everyone benefits in terms of trust, unity, teamwork and sense of commitment for themselves. Some winners based on an annual average are given overseas trips to visit some affiliated companies to learn more on how they practice and maintain and sustain 5 S. These will give them the opportunity to also share their experiences and exchange notes to improve theirs. It never stops as the innovative ideas continue to evolve as the challenges of the industry continue to push the limits of a world class manufacturing environment. So much so, everyone in the manufacturing industry are expected to adopt the highest level there is to follow and to improve from there on. Sustainability is the key to 5S success and this eventually roll up to the benefits of the company as a whole as the whole organization work with this 5S, Kaizen and Lean culture. It may take a few years to nurture and grow in strength but this is the first step to move forward with confidence in knowing that the destination will reap in great rewards in terms of company growth and profitability. Keep the momentum moving and reinforce and promote 5S continually until it becomes as natural as breathing air-keeping it lively and fresh as always. And the beauty is it keeps on going as if there is very little effort to achieve that state. It becomes part of your being and lifestyle and feels effortless and has a feel good attitude to do it for nothing. It's so natural that it becomes infectious to the people surrounding you.

DID 5S ENRICH THEIR LIFESTYLES AS WELL?

Definitely so. 5S is part of the peoples' lifestyle wherever they are- at work or at play. There is less clutter now- check out the way they park their cars in the garage, their refrigerator, their furniture, their kitchen crockery, their wardrobe, their study table, their library, their laundry, their toilets, their own dressing, their children's lifestyle as well. This is the best inheritance that they can impart onto their children- the power of empowerment and accountability to the next generation. Most of us will be working for many decades with either a corporation or maybe their own business- take this time to exercise 5S, be a real model to your neighbours, your friends, your relatives and work mates- to anybody that you have contact with or have an influence on. You would not even realise it but by the standards and discipline that you live through daily shows and affects the lifestyle of others as well. Your mere image and discipline shows in the way you speak and act out what you believe is good for you and everyone in the community.

POWERFUL TOOL:

It is a powerful tool to adopt as your new lifestyle which will only bring out the best of you which only focus on good things in life. Embrace and enjoy it as it is free. The 5S concept starts in minute steps right from the people. The Right Attitude will lead to Right Thinking and eventually Right Products and Services. We add here the Right Living. It may be simple but it's all common sense and that is why it associates well with the mass population of workers and service providers. Business is what makes a good case and a good sense to continue. It need not be filled with more complications in which it currently has- all it needs is to unclutter and make all things transparent and visual. Any non-conformance or deviation can be detected and corrected easily by whoever is closest to the issue. There is no need to wait for anyone else to take the lead as 5S promotes a likeminded community that survives synergistically.

QUESTIONS TO CHALLENGE YOURSELF

1) Wouldn't it be great to achieve something and sustain it without having to put in more effort than necessary and it carries on and on?
2) Wouldn't it be a great achievement to transform the lifestyle of yourself and your people after introducing and maintaining all the concepts of 5S?

3) Have you ever thought that you have impacted the lives of many not only in your company but also in the community by following such simple concepts of 5S?

4) Wouldn't it be great if every company and everybody in the state or country adopt this concept like what the Japanese have done?

5) Have you ever thought the moment that the Japanese World Cup spectators in Brazil did their 5S routine immediately after everyone else have left the stadium? Do you think they did it with much effort?

6) Wouldn't it be good if everyone live their lifestyle in this dignified manner and be an influence to all who are around them?

7) Isn't this a noble act and a great example to the younger generation?

8) Have you ever thought why the climbers of Mount Everest have dumped all their wastes along the way up and have never thought of retrieving their wastes on the way down? Is for their own glory to conquer Mount Everest without giving even a thought so to the pollution they have created on this beautify mountain?

5

Pareto Analysis

Pareto was a sociologist and economist who devised a 80/20 rule principle to determine the issues related to a social problem experienced in Italy at that time. His principle clearly grouped the contributing factors and gathered data through a mass survey and charted out the frequencies of each factor. He saw the trend and the crux of the problem were grouped within the total 80% of all the contributing factors. He used this principle effectively and solved the problems in a more constructive and effective manner.

In modern times, it is referred to as the **Pareto Analysis.**

It can best be explained with an actual example. Let's pick a quality problem of a product. The steps to take to derive to a solution thro Pareto Analysis:

1. Gather at least 6 months of quality defect data from all sources- from suppliers' incoming data; process quality data; outgoing quality data and customer warranty data.
2. Group similar types of defects for all the captured data and there will be a tally of the number of frequency of each defect.

Let's take the case of a product which constitutes some parts that are outsourced to a local supplier and it gets supplied to a factory thru the incoming section, gets assessed and delivered to the production line to be processed further. Imagine the data is from the sub-assembled and final product including data received thru warranty claims in the last six months of supply to the market. A simple chart is done to record the frequency of each contributing factor which appear to have caused a defect on the product.

No	Contributing Factor	6 m Freq	% Contributor	Cumm. %
1	Incomplete material quantity	55	36.4	36.4
2	Surface Damages	43	28.5	64.9
3	Inconsistent lengths	28	18.5	83.4
4	Slight burrs in holes	11	7.3	90.7
5	Rusty parts	7	4.6	95.3
6	Poor packing	5	3.3	98.6
7	Mixed parts	2	1.4	100.0
8	TOTAL	151	100.0	

3. Plot a chart with the Y-axis for the frequency and the X-axis for each defect type.
4. Chart the frequency of each defect type in a vertical bar format.
5. On the right side of the chart with another Y-axis to plot the accumulative % of the contributing factors.

Applying the 80/20 principle, we see that the 80% cumulative line highlight that three out of seven factors are the vital few that need to be addressed and by taking action for these will solve 80% of the problem. For this example, the team has to focus on the following contributing factors: Insufficient quantity, Damage of surfaces and

Inconsistent lengths as the key items that the team must focus to conduct the problem solving process. As the right analysis is derived from the intensive problem solving process we shall see that the defects that initially were the Vital Few will eventually diminish as they get solved and the defect levels will be reduced. The action taken on the Vital Few contributors will give the biggest impact to 80% of the remaining contributors. It's like a round-robbin approach- attacking the Vital Few and the Trivial Many will stand out later as the Vital Few eventually. It's a continuous improvement.

Let's look at one example where a product has some quality defects and the team has gathered data collected whenever the defects were detected at the point of incoming, during the process, outgoing check and warranty claims. The frequency of occurences were tallied and put in a table for easy review and charting of the Pareto Analysis chart. This is easily done with the help of an Excel worksheet.

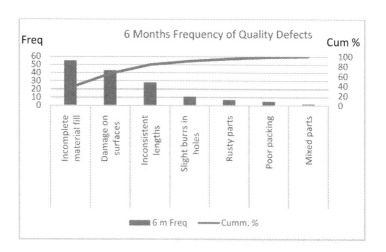

As that happens after a stretch of three months into the actions taken, another review of the data has to be done to reconstruct the Pareto charts and the earlier contributing factors which were initially considered the

Trivial Many will stand out as the next factors which will be captured under the 80% zone. Eventually each item will be addressed as it is a continuous improvement cycle. The Pareto Analysis more or less prioritise where the team should focus initially and carry on from there. It is a simple tool to use in all aspects of problem solving and it can be constructed for almost anything. Even in the service industry the contributing factors can be identified based on good data history which affects your retention issues of key customers as the external forces are always dynamic and cause a threat to your existing and future business. The simplicity of analysis appeals to any layman who always shy away from tedious and complex analysis. Nowadays such data can be easily plotted out using the Microsoft Excel worksheets that automatically plot out combo charts for immediate review with the team members. These are powerful tools which can be shared with anyone that have an interest to know the progress of the actions taken to solve the problems. It also serves as a good learning tool to educate new recruits to be involved in such activities for the betterment of their own lifestyle and also for the company that they work in. As the Vital Few contributing factors have been identified with the Pareto Analysis, then you can use several problem solving tools to analyse the data for further action. See next chapters for these problem solving tools (Fish Bone Diagram, Scatter diagram, SIPOC etc.)

QUESTIONS TO CHALLENGE YOURSELF

1) Wouldn't it be a time saver to know the priorities to work on rather than just working on any action that does not give you the maximum impact after all the hard work?

2) Wouldn't it be fun to involve yourself in this diagnostic journey to explore yourself and the potential of your team mates in finding solutions to your problems?

3) If creating charts is a big show stopper to what you want to do- then could you delegate this to your team mates or workers who are tech savvy?

4) Wouldn't this exercise open up more avenues to improve almost any issue that your customer are not happy about?

5) Wouldn't your whole supply or value chain be involved in this exercise so that the complete Value Chain will be transparent and help all processes from raw materials to the end customer to continually improve on a regular basis?

6) Wouldn't it improve your bottom line of your business?

7) Wouldn't it give you and your team a different perspective to think out of the box?

8) It will not keep you awake at night, would it, to spend quality time to address an issue that is already prioritised to solve 80% of the problem?

6

Fish Bone Brainstorming

As it is described as a Fish Bone- let's give some background as to how it came about. Having eaten a whole fish and the end of it the skeleton would normally be intact. If we reverse the process from the skeleton onwards we should be able to identify how the meat was eaten and eventually lead you to how it was eaten, cooled, prepared and from where it was caught, years in the pond, river or ocean etc. So, a Fish Bone Diagram is liken to a forensic tool that traces the origins of this fish right to the source. It's a great tool to stir up the team members who are in a brain-storming session. THE ground rules are that anyone in the team has equal rights to say anything, however idiotic or silly it can be, it does not matter as all these will be confirmed later.

Let's dissect the Fish Bone into six major structures where they will be categorized as Man, Method, Machine, Material, Money, Management, the 6Ms. These will be the main body structure where the **CAUSES** are classified and the overall **EFFECT** they have on the problem or issue as depicted by the head of the fish. Sometimes the Fish Bone diagram is often referred as the **Cause & Effect Analysis.** In order to understand the power of this problem solving tool, we shall illustrate a typical example and take you thru the various techniques on how to draw some conclusions from the brain storming sessions as probable leads or root causes. Let's familiarize ourselves with the Fish Bone diagram and focus on one particular scenario from start to finish. Let's use the previous example mentioned in the previous chapter of a product with quality defects detected from the supplier, the in-process and the warranty claims. There are six categories, 6M, to be considered for the brainstorming sessions:

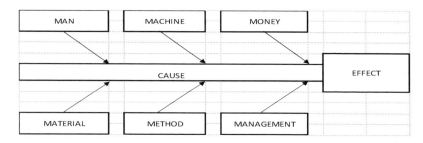

CAUSE & EFFECT ANALYSIS

Let's use the Pareto Analysis which we did awhile earlier on the quality defects of a product and the **Vital Few** contributing factors that represented more than 80% of all the factors. It is a simple compilation of data recorded over the last 6 months on the number of frequency that each contributing factor had occurred. Then each contributing factor is compared to determine whether they are the vital few or trivial many.

No	Contributing Factor	6 months Freq.	% Contributor	Cum%
1	Incomplete filled process	55	36.4	36.4
2	Surface Damages	43	28.5	64.9
3	Inconsistent lengths	28	18.5	83.4

Pick the first contributing factor 'Incomplete filled process' for one group of team members which by itself constitutes 36.4% of all the contributing factors. Leave the other two contributing factors to another two groups to handle the brainstorming. Form the team members who are in the value stream or in the area that contributed to the various processes. It may have to involve the material handler, receiving officer, supplier personnel, Quality inspector, production charge-hand and the purchasing officer. Not less than six people but can accommodate maximum of eight members in this particular effect. To Identify the **'EFFECT'** beforehand, this was discovered during the processing of the sub-assembly parts supplied from a nearby factory that is one of the company's panel of approved suppliers. The production supervisor discovered that the sub-assembly item supplied to the line had an insufficient injection of material which caused the part to be brittle and easily breaks during assembly to another part. The members in the team will undertake to have a brainstorming session using the fish bone diagram and ask the 5 Whys to reveal the probable root causes. Let's see how this can be done by going through the six categories of the Causes: (the probable root causes have been underlined in italics):

MATERIAL: refers to both incoming materials and finished goods of the supplier and main factory, respectively.

Q1) Why didn't the incoming inspector detect *the defects* on the supplier's sub-assembled parts?
A1) The incoming data *did not detect any defect* on materials supplied from the supplier and they have visited the supplier on regular basis and confirmed that their processes are in good order.

Q2) Why didn't the *Quality inspectors capture* the finished goods defect?
A2) It was *difficult to inspect* the final produced as the outer molding surface *prevents any chance to inspect this defect visually*.

Q3) Why didn't the Quality department *invest in soft x-ray* machines to inspect regular samples? Or outsource this capability?

A3) Our *company do not have such expensive machines* but we *do oursource* some samples to the outside labs to inspect *but is not regularly done* because it was expensive to do so.

Q4) Why didn't the company *institute a regular destructive tests* to cut up the molded parts and do a regular inspection?

A4) It was *done before* and since the inspectors did not find any defects, they *have stopped* at the instruction of management, in order *to save costs.*

Q5) Why wasn't the *savings* on such important inspection not *compared* to the total cost of poor quality products like machine downtime, process defects, extra hours and materials to rework and loss of sales opportunities due to substandard products?

A5) *Top management do not appear to be worried* as the demand exceeds supply for the moment. This is always the case for quick decisions to park this issue till it blows up later when the economy is down.

MAN: refers to the Production worker

Q1) Why didn't the worker *set up the injection machine* as per the standard parameters for this type of product?

A1) The worker did not make any reference to the standard charts as he *just took over the shift from his colleague* and had assumed that there should not be any problem to continue as is.

Q2) Why didn't the Quality inspector perform a *sample check* during the shift change?

A2) It was done but not at the beginning of shift change but rather about *an hour later, which is as per the inspection schedule.*

Q3) Why was it *predetermined* that the inspection should be done based on time rather than based on production output?
A3) This was *predetermined by the engineer many years ago* and *have not updated* the production set up and inspection parameters since the factory started.

Q4) Why isn't the engineer involved in the monthly production output schedule so that he could have adjusted the inspection frequency based on production rate rather than on time of day or week?
A4) *Most of key personnel are not invited* to discuss on a regular basis and this is reason of the non-updates of standards and policies.

Q5) Why is that so?
A5) The Plant manager have empowered the production planning to the scheduler and *did not encourage group meetings*.

MACHINE: refers to the Injection molding machine for final product

Q1) Why was this part not being detected during molding?
A1) There are ten cavities in each mold and the speed of the molding is too quick. *Some defects do happen but comes on and off*.

Q2) Why didn't the worker feedback to the supervisor to get the technician to inspect the mold to determine which cavity is defective?
A2) There is only one mold that makes this particular part and the *production schedule is very tight every month and it cannot be shut down at any day to inspect the mold.*

Q3) Why didn't the production scheduler plan the capacity to include time for mold and machine inspection?

A3) The scheduler do not spend time discussing with the maintenance, engineering and _production planning department was scheduled as deemed fit without consultation from stake-holders._

Q4) Why didn't the Plant Manager get involved to consider all the production and maintenance parameters before approving the production schedule?
A4) There was no need for him to approve the production schedule as _he was always busy in other activities_, like sales, financing and marketing activities.

MANAGEMENT: refers to the organization of the factory

Q1) Why didn't the Plant manager set aside time to review the monthly SIOP (Sales, Inventory, Operations and Planning) meetings?
A1) This factory is a family owned business and the _Plant manager is not competent to lead this company_ as a highly qualified professional as he rose from rank and file.

Q2) Why didn't top management invest in more molding machines after knowing that sales had picked up over the months?
A2) The present factory cannot accommodate more molding machines as the _current factory space and layout cannot take in more machinery._

Q3) Why didn't top management foresee all these constraints?
A3) _They have no idea of capacity and machinery planning._ They practice adhoc decision making and its rather messy.

Q4) Why didn't top management employ more competent staff to perk up the in-competencies of the various critical operational issues?
A4) Being a family business the _top management prefer to position family members to fill in the gap_ regardless of their competence or skills.

Q5) Why didn't the staff and workers make suggestions to top management on what needs to be done to fix key issues faced by them?

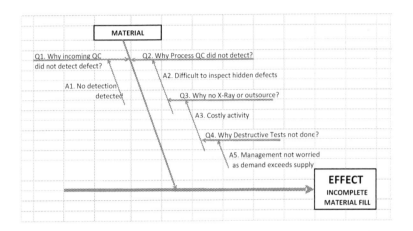

A5) Currently *there is no forum or any Kaizen activities* to allow the staff and workers to participate in problem solving sessions.

Out of the six categories, from the example of the brainstorming that touches on only four, it is quite evident that the root causes really stood out as the 5 Whys penetrated some pertinent questions to get to the bottom of the root cause.

The above 5 Whys Q&A normally is scribbled and charted out into a pictorial Fish-Bone diagram. To illustrate this, we use the 5 Whys on the MATERIALS category to give you a visual representation:

From the above brainstorming session- we can deduce the root cause from each category as follows:

MATERIAL: It was established that the incoming material or supplier's sub-assembled parts were acceptable and the defect actually originated from the final molding process of our factory.

Probable Root Cause: The quality department did not have any device to check hidden defects after final assembly and did not perform regular destructive tests to inspect the finished goods even though they have not discovered anything amiss in the earlier years.

MAN: It was established that the worker did not refer to the standard machine set up procedures for many years already.

Probable Root Cause: The engineer, supervisor, worker and quality inspectors appear to have taken the processes for granted not knowing the impact of their in-competencies and grave assumptions of the processes.

MACHINE: It was established that the worker did not feedback the issues with some of the bad cavities from the mold die and Maintenance was not able to stop the machine to check the mold.

Probable Root Cause: The production scheduler had planned the daily or monthly production schedule in isolation of the real situation of the condition of the machines, mold dies, quality inspection intervals, machine downtime and inspection time etc. The machines were running at almost 100% of its capacity.

MANAGEMENT: It was established that the management lack the core competence in the most critical processes of the business.

Probable Root Cause: Being a family business, it is rather difficult to look outside for talents and still depends on the resources of the family even though they may not be competent or skilled enough to watch over the critical aspects of the business. Based on the above probable causes that gave rise to the effect of 'Insufficient quantity of materials or under filled molding' we can redefine the few probable causes more clearly by assigning the members to confirm the various assumptions, opinions or hunches as to what the real or root causes are. This is the Diagnostic Confirmation to determine actions that will create a great impact.

The questions asked have to be wide but penetrating and any lead should be further questioned. Focus on:

- Questioning the Questions
- Questioning the Answers
- Answering the Questions

Don't leave anything unquestioned so that every angle is covered by the team members. Most of the answers given will not have any substance or proof of the answer but this is left to the second stage where the Diagnostic Confirmation plan comes into play to filter out all these bias and unclear comments and opinions. Keep the team motivated and don't let them feel that their feedback is not important. The message is to emphasise on continuous improvements and their views will be considered eventually.

From the Fish Bone Diagram- review each item and single out the most probable root causes, circle them as you will revisit them for the next step. Do not strike out those opinions until the Diagnostic Confirmation Plan is completed and conclusive. In this manner the continuous process of elimination of trivial opinions will fizzle out and the vital few root causes will stand out where further action need to be taken to address the root cause.

The Leader will summarise the first findings and table the most probable causes and identify the members to take responsibility to confirm the actual status of the causes and set a time frame to complete the confirmation. Involve all members to support the data gathering and on-site confirmation of items identified by the team members. Appoint the person in-charged to get those items done within the time frame committed by them.

The data is tabulated for easy monitoring by the team members. The objective is to confirm the situation at site and to report the findings in the net meeting for further deliberation and alternative actions. The option to either KIV or drop the original assumptions lies with the decision of the team leader so that the resources can focus on more probable leads based on the feedback of the findings at site.

Stick to the plan and adjust accordingly after each confirmation. Do not change the plan until the situation is confirmed so as to take one step at a time to eliminate all the probable causes.

However, don't discount the items that appear to be not important now but could be revisited as the process gets going. The history is important for training purposes and also it reflects the maturity of all team members who can later be coached to lead other groups at the shop floor level.

Use these real examples during the early formative weeks when inducting new employees into the company. Have the new teams review past projects so that they can have a feel of how the earlier groups went thru the same motions as what they are going thru so that they can have a bigger picture of the journey taken by their earlier counterparts.

Below is the Diagnostic confirmation plan for the team to follow-up.

DIAGNOSTIC CONFIRMATION PLAN

Category / Probable Root Cause	Assigned to Team member	When
MATERIAL - Check the past year's data of destructive tests (% failure rates and the reason of failures)	Quality inspector	1 week
MAN - Track the frequency of Engineering or Quality Change Notices since the operations started (No. of changes and why they were changed?)	Engineer	1 week
MACHINE - Track the number of meetings held by the production scheduler, production, maintenance supervisor and Plant on monthly production plan (number of meetings and attendance records etc)	Production supervisor	1 week
MANAGEMENT - Track and chart out the organization chart and map out the current Job descriptions of all management, supervisory and charge-hand responsibility	Plant manager	1 week

Various data gathering and analysis tools will be discussed in later chapters to assist your team members to complete the Diagnostic Confirmation Plan with factual and constructive data. This will lead the team to focus further and continue to data-mine until the truth is revealed. The truth of the real root cause is important to be determined so that the subsequent wasteful events or activities can be eliminated once and for all. This is the path to a cleaner and leaner operations without unnecessary clutter in the operational and management processes which actually takes a lot of time off the current work force and whole organisation.

If you don't already have your teams prepared to accept reality and be brave to speak up during the brain storming sessions, then, it is high time to do so. The culture of honest and truthful feedback is enabled in these forums where the opinions or suggestions raised are with respect to the issue and not directed to any persons or authorities in the company.

Certain rules apply during these brainstorming sessions and must be respected by all members, be it they are the authorities or top management or not- in these meetings everyone is equal to speak up without fear or favour. To solve the root cause we must get deep into hidden secrets that must be set free. Moreover, any hunches or assumptions will be fact checked using this Diagnostic Confirmation Plan so as to put to rest non-factual contributors so that work that is done later is not wasted but will add value to the final results that will come thru constructive actions and activities carried out by the team members themselves. At the end of it trust in one another w ll be developed and teamwork will be enhanced in the company. It is not only one group of problem solvers but eventually it will expand throughout. You will be surprised to know that some corporations that have started from humble beginnings have growing pains when it grew too fast and the company identity appears to be vague as more hires from other companies and work culture were put into the corporate melting pot and expected them to gel into a homogeneous power team. Sadly, it is not that simple. It takes time. It is not impossible but slightly difficult. Use these problem solving tools to tear those silos that are protecting their ego- set them loose in the safe environment of problem solving and you will be surprised of the power and energy in your teams. Use this synergy to assist you to empower your team to take ownership and commitment to undertake the activities themselves. Let them know how their actions have contributed to the solutions and reward them either with a 'Good Job' or Handshake at the end of the project. Let them walk into these sessions and walk away feeling great inside that they have add value into the problem solving sessions and have also contributed to the improved bottom line of the company.

7

Scatter Charts

It is quite uncommon to use scatter charts unless your team encounter some issues where the problem appears to be scattered in different parts of the product, processes or different locations of your services. It is more of a visual aid to see the extent or magnitude of the issue.

In the Medical Field: For the case of the recent EBOLA virus endemic in affected regions of West Africa, we may not appreciate how widespread this virus is until we see it in a visual format that indicates some severity of this outbreak in terms of number of deaths, enduring victims and potential risk areas.

The scatter diagram is best used to indicate the direction of the spread of the disease. See the example below of an EBOLA outbreak:

Pictorially, anyone can comprehend the severity of EBOLA outbreak when the number of cases and deaths encountered in each affected region is recorded and monitored to contain the situation. And with this scatter chart, the medical team are able to mobilize whatever resources they may have to the precise area of need. Proper medication can be despatched on time and in the quantities needed. Even location of burial or cremation sites can be plotted in the above chart to appreciate the location of the burial sites of all victims.

In the manufacturing sector: Scatter charts are widely used to identify and monitor the effects of countermeasures on chronic problems. Automotive body painting defects on painted body finishes are usually audited with scatter charts at the outgoing area before the vehicle gets trimmed with interior parts. The scatter charts will have a pre-drawn shape of the vehicle body showing areas of the top side, left and right sides and the front and rear sides. The painting inspector will use a marker to tick off the areas of the painted surface if he finds dirt, scratches or dents on the vehicles. For each type of defect, he uses a different symbol. The same chart will be populated for at least 10 vehicles to understand the trend of the defects and the area of the body that has this issue. With this audit on a daily basis, the body shop and painting shop Kaizen team will be able to investigate and take appropriate actions to minimize and/or eliminate the chronic problem. As this audit is continuously performed as part of the painting process- the customers will not see such defects the moment he or she receives the new vehicle.

The inspector has marked the defects inflicted on the painted surface of the vehicle. Each symbol represents a particular type of defect collected over a certain population of painted bodies for the team to take further action and the results of the countermeasure will be measure again to confirm the effectiveness. It will continue until the target of acceptable quality level has been fulfilled. This audit need not be prolonged as long the paintshop engineers are able to pinpoint the root cause of the problem and the frequency of inspection can be reduced to a confident level that zero defects are possible. This tool definitely eliminates waste and add value to better painted cars that do not require further rework on freshly painted surfaces so as to retain its original state and not aggravate or expose such rework area to the mercy of the environment, the sun, acid rain and other contaminants. The actions taken are also related to good Total Preventative Maintenance of equipment and tools in any manufacturing facility.

In the Service sector: Scatter charts are normally used to compare prices of second-hand goods. For example- used cars may show the prices appear to be lower for standard or common models and age; whereas the vintage cars may appear to fetch higher prices as they age.

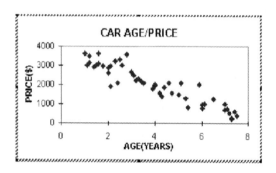

Scatter charts can also monitor the cost of repairs of new and older vehicles- as they age and are constantly used on the road, the more it cost to keep them running. This chart can make the owner to decide whether to sell off this vehicle or purchase a new one based on the scatter chart data.

Scatter charts can also capture the distribution centers of your business in terms of revenue and size of the market. This will help you decide on whether to expand or maintain or shutdown that particular outlet as it could have constrained your workforce and budget to continue to service that sector and region.

Scatter charts can also monitor the location of ATM machines that your company has supplied to each bank and it also can record the occurrences of ATM breakdowns daily or weekly or monthly. This will allow the team to determine the root causes of whether it is due to abuse of machine (because of the neighborhood) or a machine defect.

It can get creative to include the frequency of ATM usage (monitored remotely via web-link) to predetermine the preventative maintenance needed for the printing mechanism, software upgrade and general servicing of the consumable parts so as to prevent adhoc calls from the bank in the odd hours of the day and week. This tools aids to eliminate waste by focusing on value-add activities that benefits both the company and the end user. It also eliminates the need to have huge stocks of spare parts way ahead of the expiry dates of the duty cycles. It saves time and effort for the customer and also yourself and everybody will be very productive in every activity.

8

SIPOC Charts

The SIPOC chart can briefly be described as a series of competitive lanes of a swimming pool. In this case it has five lanes and separated by anti-splash floaters so that they will not create water ripples caused within each lane by the other swimmers. Similarly the SIPOC chart is represented by five swimmers:

S- Sales;

I - Incoming materials;

P- Procurement;

O- Operations and

C- Customers

All the above have their own parameters to safeguard so as to reach the goal of winning the race. And to do that all the disturbances in the other lanes must be minimized as not to interrupt by causing ripples across the lanes. So, with the SIPOC chart, you should be able to identify the ripples that create non-value add elements to the total race.

SIPOC charts need not be limited to identify- the processes that are relevant to your business or work process. It may include alternative elements of a service counter of a fast food counter where we can identify it as C-Customer choice; C-Customer Relations; C- Cooking Process; C-Capacity; C-Complaints or in short a **5C** Chart if you want to assess the non-value add ripples. The elements of the chart is flexible to serve your requirements.

Let's go through an example on what the SIPOC chart can reveal the situation of a manufacturing problem:

First of all, formalize your team from the related processes- in this case the Sales Manager, Warehouse Manager, Purchasing staff, Operations Manager and Customer (Warranty Claims) officer. Facilitate via a brain storming as described in earlier chapters- after validating the suspected circumstances- list them down in accordance to the areas of responsibility. That's what we are getting at- who and what caused the ripples to the other swimmers.

No	Suppliers	Incoming	Purchasing	Operations	Customer
1	Late orders received	Short shipment	Adhoc purchase orders	Mis-scheduling issues	Delays in deliveries
2	New Prices not confirmed	Quality defects	Alternative sourcing	Poor output yields	Deliveries rejected
3	Delays in outsourced	Items arrived at odd hours	Short order on key items	Dimensional issues	Items - Functional
4	Workers sick leave	Unplanned storage racks	Error in part numbers	Mistake in m/c set up	Customer complaints
5	etc	etc	etc	etc	etc

The above chart clearly identify the issues encountered by each department in the company. Some of the issues identified may not have originated from that department as it could be contributed by other departments. On this particular example, the Purchasing department could be the one that is causing ripples across the whole value stream of the company.

Let's attempt to determine the next example in the restaurant kitchen:

No	Customer Choice	Customer Relations	Cooking Process	Capacity	Customer complaints
1	Prolonged Browse of menu	Unable to Sell and Upsell	Wrong cooking sequence	First In-First Out ignored	Dishes jumped queue
2	Over order-cancellations	Over sold dishes	Slow to cook dishes	Inexperienced cook	Long waiting time
3	Unhappy with dish	Poor recommendatio	Too much salt or sauce	Erratic estimations	Dissatisfied with taste
4	Changed booked orders	Delayed delivery of dishes	Missed one order	Difficulty to read orders	Upset customers
5	etc	etc	etc	etc	etc

Which process do you think created the most ripples to the rest of the kitchen flow? We could eliminate at least two processes that are related to the customers (Customer Choice and Customer Complaints)- applying the golden rule that the Customer is Always Right – we are left with three processes (Customer Relations, Cooking Process and Capacity).

It's obvious that the Customer Relations (usually called the Captain) has pushed or upsold more dishes than what the customer and guests could consume. It could be a bad mix of too much bulky meat and expensive dishes.

The cooks in the kitchen are always busy and working like machines. The golden rule of rubbish in- rubbish out applies here as well. If the Customer Relations staff has a horrible handwriting that the cook (who prepares the items) could have misread- he may not have the time to verify but go ahead and cook it and deal with it later.

Not all cooks have the same taste levels- as most of them use gut and feel and also their tongues as a benchmark to estimate the level of saltiness of the dish. No such thing as one teaspoonful of salt or sugar – that is the problem. At least some form of special utensils are provided, then, there will be some form of standardization- like what chefs in Hotel chains are practicing as they have very high standards to deal with elite customers from around the world. You may not agree on this observation but one man's medicine is another man's poison.

Having known where the biggest ripples are from, then, form a team to conduct an open brainstorming session and adopt the Root Cause Analysis (RCA) to zoom into probable issues, which are covered in earlier chapters, to get to the root cause and validate all the assumptions and probable contributors and take the appropriate action to get these ripples removed. The deeper the issues are addressed by the team the better the process flow and operations. Use the tools mentioned in earlier chapters and approach the issues in a systematic manner and you will derive at your answers sooner than you have thought about it.

Allow your team to contribute by expressing their thoughts and allow them to take ownership of the issues. This is a sure way of getting the team to work cohesively to resolve their daily issues. Make it fun and they will eventually like this idea and sustain the momentum as they see real results from their actions.

9

Value Stream Mapping

Now that you have started off adopting the 5S concept and is on your way to unclutter your work place and private lifestyle, then, you are ready to continue your Lean journey with Value Stream Mapping aka VSM. This approach appears to be the most misinterpreted topic in all Lean concepts. To the procurement officer it may mean a Supply Chain Network, to a Service provider its supplying a unique service, to a layman it may mean a stream of activities that has value. Some of it is true but most of it is incorrect.

In simple terms it only means identifying the areas of your processes where it lacks integration of value added activities. There are many ways to look at VSM and also there are many approaches to conducting a VSM. After having analysed many scenarios in many industries over the years, It has been found that the easier way is not to follow the technical approach but to use common sense and some of the VSM principles. The technical approach is too difficult to comprehend if you are not tech savvy. It may be unorthodox to say but it is quite effective and quicker to derive to the same results. We shall limit the use of familiar acronyms of VA- Value Add, NVA- Non Value Add or CT-Cycle Time and IT- Idle Time.

These acronyms cannot be torn apart and interpreted in another way as they are the core elements to look for in any VSM analysis. We will take an easier path so that anybody in the work place of home can do it with ease. There are various steps that one have to follow and review it with the team until all the needed information and data are fulfilled for a good analysis to take the next course of action to resolve the problems and issues that currently plaguing you and your team members, not mentioning your customers as well.

Remember these simple steps and you will not go wrong:

- B: Brainstorming session to assess the processes - 1 hour
- V: On-site verification- 2 hours
- A: Action Plan- to streamline processes- 1 hour
- R: Review results On-site and adjust to suit- 1 week later

That is all we need to do together with your team or stakeholders that are associated either directly or indirectly with the processes. What the above BVAR is only focusing on is the collaboration of a core team, focusing on the processes to unleash the bottleneck or eliminate the non-value add activities.

VSM charts spanning the whole meeting room, putting in data which really are very subjective and not tangible can be utilized but may appear too technical as processing data are needed. What the team needs is a real on-site observation and a brain storming session. From the initial observation and brainstorming at least everyone is on the same page to put forward their views and proposals and also to focus on the flow of the processes- including data information and material flow. The basic data will be on process Cycle Time (CT), Idle Time (IT), Distance between Processes (DBP).

PROCESS TIME: This is the actual time taken for work to be done on the item or product.

IDLE TIME: This is equivalent to the time where there is no work done on the product even though the machine is alright. Either the worker is waiting for parts that never arrived on time or the preceeding item had a quality issue.

CYCLE TIME: For every process the cycle time needs to be clocked with a stop watch for at least six cycles. After clocking for a string of six cycles, take the average time per cycle by dividing the total accumulated recorded time by the number of cycles accumulated. The Cycle Time is the total sum of the Process including the Idle Time. To be more accurate to time the Cycle time- it is best to observe and time at least 3 cycles and take an average figure obtained from an average worker. This is good enough for a start.

DISTANCE BETWEEN PROCESSES: The distances that the parts had to be transported or conveyed from one process to another plays an important part to the total productivity of the processes. In most cases machinery are scattered throughout the factory rather than being grouped in work cells to minimize or eliminate unnecessary movements and transfers.

TYPICAL VSM CHART: Since VSM is a collective state of affairs of comparing the Value-add and Non-Value-add activities of all the processes, it is classified into the assessment of the CURRENT STATE and the preferred FUTURE STATE. We shall make a study of a typical factory producing a plastic injection part for the automotive industry.

CURRENT STATE: Let's get accustomed to the standard VSM symbols that are commonly used during brain-storming of the complete processes. You can include other symbols for easy mapping and discussion as it depends on your type of business and service. The processes are mapped out as it is and the lines are of two types- the bold lines are for material or services flow and the dotted lines are for data flow.

Map out the processes in the simplest form and not to include non-relevant sub processes which do not have much impact on the overall value stream. It be included later if the early investigations require that to be included as a bottleneck.

Use A1 sized paper flip charts to map out the process as this will be kept to track all mappings and discussion points or highlights on this piece of paper. IT has to be archive later for future follow-up meetings.

Do not strike out or erase original markings- leave it as a record of the thought trail. The brain storming session is important as it will be reviewed to make it less cluttered as the team gets more involved in the discussions. The ultimate objective is to get the team members to collaborate and trust one another as one team. This is a subtle way to tear down barriers of silo thinking and bringing everyone in the offices and working floor into the open.

This is how the open office concept works- no silos, no barriers and no hierarchy that induce a collaborative and friendly environment to help one another, no emails or phone calls, just a verbal and eye to eye conversation or instruction.

This is what we missed nowadays with the advanced state of multi social media communications that are so impersonal. At times, emails are used even when the two communicators are sitting side by side. How impersonal can you get when this happens on the personal and business level?

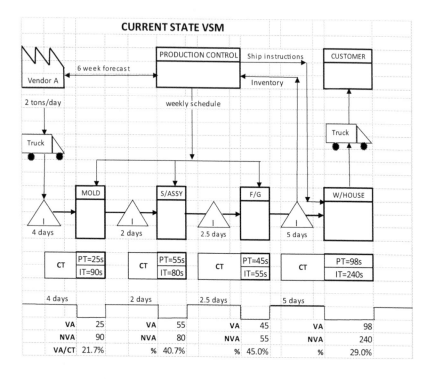

CURRENT STATE VSM

For the Current State VSM- we show a scenario where the value-add ratio is rather low. From the above data the VA (Value Add) ratio versus the Total Cycle Time appears to be erratic for each process in view of the different Process and Idle Times, hence accumulating high levels of inventory between processes. In this case study, the overall VA % is 32.4 %. This is not a pretty picture as a lot of non-value add areas are evident throughout the total process. A target should be set to achieve at least 65% Value Add. This is the first target and eventually should be improved further as the initial issues are resolved eventually and the situation is more stable to take the next course of action. Continuous improvement is the key to getting to the root of the issue and getting the maximum out of all the efforts put into the project or initiatives.

FUTURE STATE:

After the brain-storming, focus on the bottlenecks created by the Production Control and the processes that are placed far apart. For this case study it was found that the sub- assembly and final assembly operations could actually be incorporated into one machine rather than split the processes as it involves extra WIP build up and also great distances to transfer and man-handle the materials and parts.

The team will take the next step to Plan, Do, Check and take Corrective Action (PDCA) based on the above direction decided by the team leader and members.

P- Planning
D- Doing
C- Checking, and
A- Action or Alternative action.

The projected WIP reduction and Process Time adjustments expected will determine the FUTURE state of the VSM.

PLANNING: The goal of the planning stage is to get from the CURRENT to the FUTURE state. Plan the relayout to incorporate the sub-assembly and final assembly processes. This will eliminate the WIP stock level and the machine can be unified to perform two processes simultaneously. The material racks can be combined in a single location for easy access. The savings in worker movement is also possible as the material-worker and machine zones are within reach.

Remember the simple tools of Lean (5S, One Piece Flow, SMED, TPM, On-Time Delivery, Zero Defect etc) and apply them together with your team members. You have to get going. Planning is all about setting up the Team (people from the areas of concern) and getting their full commitment to work on the activities:-

MEASURABLE GOALS: Having known the quantum of the issue you are now able to determine the FUTURE state. Pre-determine a target that will give you an impact of a 50% improvement. In this manner the activities directed to these targets will be Specific, Measureable, Actionable, Reliable and Time Based, in short it's **S M A R T.** Having determined the Future State with a set goal – then you are ready for the next cycle.

DOING: "**Brain storming Session**". Organise the team members for a brainstorming session which is part of the **Root Cause Analysis (RCA).** This will be covered extensively in the next chapter but will be briefly stated here. This is a forum where everyone gets a chance to voice out their assumptions, presumptions, thoughts, opinions, unproven statements or even to keep quiet. Every point raised will be checked and verified with some initial investigative actions. This has to be done on site. We shall cover the **Gemba Kaizen ("On-site Verification")** in later portions of this book as the investigation also involves on-site Kaizen improvements to get to the root cause.

After the verification the real action to address the contributing factors that created the issue will be identified clearly bearing in mind SMART and to identify the team members to carry out the action and do the followup.

CHECK: ("Review Results") After allowing some time for the initial actions to take place, send out the same team to make another evaluation of the results based on the actions taken. Gather the data and see the trends. IF the improvement is non evident, then the team has to decide to improve upon or abandon the initial action. More data can be requested if the initial one did not portray the correct trouble spot and new indicators can also be introduced to monitor the progress of the new actions.

ACTION: This portion works together with the CHECK portion. They reciprocate with one another until there is a change in state of the issue. The timing taken is dependent on the complexity of the contributing factors and also full commitment of the team which may be enlarged to include assistance from outside the existing team members. External help may be needed if the problem becomes too technical and the present team members will not be able to handle it effectively. In this case they will take directions from the external partners and collaborate to execute some actions and continue with the data collection.

KEEP IT SIMPLE: Pick on issues that follow SMART. The whole cycle of PDCA should take longer than three months to complete the first cycle. Usually it takes three cycles before the real root cause is finally nailed and stay nailed. It is a good practice to document such successes and have it catalogued for future reference and also provide a resource for training purposes. As the situation sustain its FUTURE state, then standardize the activities and roll them up to review the current SOPs and keep it update in all training of new recruits, existing workers and externally to suppliers and service providers. Contain the situation and move forward in a continuous manner as PDCA and the rest of the tools used for Lean development is always dynamic and changing daily.

Continue to focus on the Future State to meet the goal of an overall Value-add of 65%. As described below in the chart the small continuous changes to the daily schedule and incorporation of processes have improved the Value-add of the VSM. Keep everything simple and not to add complicated processes that will confuse the human mind and eventually the manpower will just take short cuts and omit some pertinent processes which will result in more problems for the preceding and succeeding processes. Learning from past experience- keep the essential processes and cut off the rest.

Monitor the changes as a result of the various actions taken. Slight adjustments are normal after such drastic actions. The team must be ever-ready to advise and feedback any change of behaviors of the operators or old habits that could not be easily de-learned to accept the new changes. These are to be reported on daily basis to the team leader so that it could be dealt with immediately.

Simplification is key to make the future state workable- not to create more confusion to the people in the process- they must feel happy to have this new change so that any future changes will be well accepted. The old saying goes that Die -hards are difficult to change must not creep in. Make new layouts to look different, even colors, orientation of the machine and seating positions should be changed so as to refresh the older workers and re-train them as if they have just been recruited and they should feel so as well- treated as a new worker. This is a refreshing feeling for the older worker and their attitudes and habits will change for the better. They will be happier and thus contribute to better productivity and better quality of products. Keep their work attitudes positive, take their suggestions into consideration and implement them- this will encourage them to contribute even more to themselves, to their peers and to the company. Recognise their good contributions with monthly awards etc.

FUTURE STATE VSM

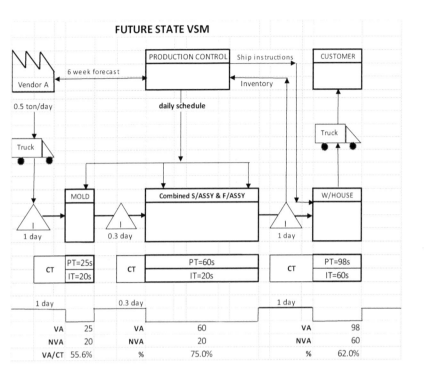

QUESTIONS TO CHALLENGE YOURSELF

1) Is it that difficult to form a workout session and thrash out ideas from the team members to identify the Value-add and Non-Value add areas?

2) In VSM analysis, do we only focus on the value-add ratio of each process and work from there?

3) What if the Future State goals are too far off and not achievable?

4) Are you well versed with the SMART action planning?

5) Are you able to evaluate and drop off irrelevant processes and declutter the total process?

6) Are you listening to your people on the current processes and bothered to take a look at it to validate that important feedback and make an important change or drop the process?

10

Root Cause Analysis

RCA, in short, adopt certain techniques to unveil the real issues. Apart from the usual brainstorming technique, here we will focus on the few that are favorites of manufacturing facilities. Most of it require only a few members from the concerned or affected areas together with a dedicated facilitator.

The method looks at six areas that can cause the problem to an issue. They are Man, Method, Machine, Materials, Management and Money. The 6 Ms as they are commonly known n the industry. These are the areas to look for root causes to a problem. They are sometimes interrelated on one way or another. Some can be independent by itself and that itself affects 80% of the issue.

This Cause and Effect analysis will need to ask 'why' at least six times and usually it is at this stage that the root cause will be determined. Why is this possible? Each question moves deeper each time an answer is revealed- like a redirection for the next line of questioning which is similar to a court case where the lawyer probes the areas he or she thinks is a probable area to dive and penetrate the barriers and unveil the truth of the situation. Take an example of a hypothetical issue, say, a car knocked into another vehicle at the traffic lights. Whoever that is involved or even as onlookers will blabber away all sorts of questions to determine who is at fault. At the end of it nobody is the wiser as it's all based on hearsays and eye-witness accounts which have yet to be validated as the truth or not. This is what Root Cause Analysis is all about- to determine the real truth of the matter and to validate the various assumptions

The series of questions asked will go like this:

FREAK ACCIDENTS ON THE ROAD

1. Why didn't the drivers see each other before they cross the junction?
   a. **Answer:** the other driver has the right of way because the lights were green. It is the other driver who ran the lights
2. Why did the driver run the lights even when it was red?
   a. **Answer:** the driver was speeding and was not familiar with the road as he was from outstation.
3. Why didn't the driver slow down his vehicle as he approached the junction?
   a. **Answer:** The driver was very tired and did not appear to be alert at that time
4. Why the driver was tired and not alert?
   a. **Answer:** The driver drove for many hours and did not have enough sleep.
5. Why did he not rest and refresh himself at the various stops before coming into the town?
   a. **Answer:** The driver was afraid to stop as the last gas station was very remote and he was out of cash at the same time

6. Then why didn't he prepare enough cash or prepare his credit card before-hand and not get into this trouble?
   a. **Answer:** It was an emergency as he was actually heading along the highway but had to divert to this town to fill up his petrol tank.

So from the six questions and answers given, what do you think was the root cause of the accident? It may be a multiple reason but they are all interrelated. First of all he came out as an emergency to somewhere, he did not prepare enough cash or bring his credit card and his car petrol ran out before he could get to the next petrol station along the highway.

In another example where most manufacturing facilities face are usually related to quality of components, the line of questioning maybe more technical but more or less in the line of questioning to reveal the truth:

MANUFACTURING DEFECTS

1. Why do we have 40% rejection rate on this item and continue to be so for the rest of the month?
   a. **Answer**: The quality inspector has been very vigilant and continue to focus on this non-compliance
2. Why wasn't the repetitive quality issue highlighted to the Engineering and Production department to shut it down?
   a. **Answer**: The production supervisor was rushing this order as the dateline is near and he resorted to keep the machine running and sort out the bad ones at a later stage
3. Why didn't Quality department shut down the machine?
   a. **Answer**: The quality department actually reports to the Production manager and so the direction from production

manager was to continue the production regardless of the poor quality.

4. Why didn't the quality department report this situation to the Plant manager as he can stop this operation

a. **Answer:** There is not much interest shown by the Plant manager to reprimand the production manager as he trusted him to produce and does not want to get involved.

5. Why didn't the finance department issue a rework and recall hours calculation in-order to highlight this issue during the monthly staff meeting?

Such details are usually discussed by the Plant manager and in most cases the real issues are not highlighted for fear of retaliation and bad office politics. Why didn't quality department highlight the seriousness of the goods returned so far to reflect the true situation of quality and customer complaints?

Answer: No such forum was encouraged by the top management.

Very clearly here, the top management are not interested to manage the issues- it could be a fear of having to replace some machinery or tooling and also to appease the political situation of the company.

This is bad as the customer will one day snap back to demand that their products at least meet the minimum standards or else they will source elsewhere.

POOR SERVICE AT FAST FOOD OUTLET

1. Why did the customer complained of poor service at the outlet?

a. **Answer:** He was not satisfied with the long wait at the counter to get his order as he was in a hurry to hit the highway.

2. What did he order that required such a long wait and why wasn't he proposed an alternative meal?

a. **Answer:** The counter helper was new and this was his first day at work and that could be the reason for not proposing an alternative meal to speed up the service.

3. Why was the counter helper not being mentored or supervised on the first day of work, where was the supervisor?

a. **Answer:** The supervisor was supposed to guide the new employee at the counter but because of an absent counter helper, the supervisor had to fill in that post as well.

4. How is it that this outlet attrition rate is deteriorating and affecting the speed of speed of service?

a. **Answer:** There was insufficient support given by the owner of this outlet and also the supervisor has some issues with motivating his staff and counter helpers to perform their work well. This has contributed to poor attendance of his support staff.

5. What has the supervisor and the owner of this outlet done to remedy the situation?

a. **Answer:** Nothing.

The above situation has highlighted some probable causes that lead to the current state of the service level of this fast food outlet. The management and supervisors appear to be firefighting the situation as and when the counter helpers either resign or do not turn up for work on a regular basis. They do not have any strategy to retain the present work force. I believe there was not enough empathy on the part of the supervisor to listen out to the issues that his workers may be facing- he needs to listen and find out what are the issues. The root cause here is that both the supervisor and the top management do not appear to entertain two way communication to improve the operations and service level as this affects the attention that need to be given to their customers.

If we did not perform this simple Root Cause Analysis, the blame is always on the poor performance and tardiness of the workers. But, with the series of prying questions, we are able to pinpoint a probable root cause in the management style of this outlet. And if the appropriate actions are put in place, then, this outlet will definitely recover its status as a well run fast food service provider and the customers will be happy to patronize it regularly without much complaints. The issue may be trivial but it hits the pockets of the consumers. Why call it fast food if the customer could not it as advertised. They are not interested in what or why they it can happen but they are more interested in a fast service as they are either too hungry or in a hurry to get to somewhere urgently. Over here the question of a weak backroom support needs to be strengthened or outsourced to professionals. All the nitty gritty of interviewing and hiring competent staff will be taken care of and the chances of having one bad apple slip through the selection process will be minimal and will not affect the unpleasant front desk encounter with the customers. We don't need this kind of attitudes when it can be prevented right from the start. The front counter represents the face of your company and reflects its corporate identity and for what it stands for. Customers perceive all employees to stand up and be proud of what they themselves believe in. It also gives pride to the customers that they also associate their good judgment and decision to buy the products. So, imagine how disappointed they will be if they encountered such pleasantries.

QUESTIONS TO CHALLENGE YOURSELF

1) Don't everybody want to solve the problem and have solved once and for all?

2) If the number of questions that need to be asked during the brainstorming are not asked then, don't you think these will be asked later when the same problem repeats itself later on?

3) Wouldn't it be better to get all the questions asked in the beginning so that the team members can have the total perspective of the issue to make a good decision to derive a better result?

4) Wouldn't it save a lot of time in the end as the team can focus on each phase of the problem solving- mobilizing all the resources and focus on one aspect at a time?

5) Wouldn't it be good to nail all probable causes that lead to the final effect of the problem and have proper documentation to standardize the work that will eliminate these root causes once and for all?

6) Wouldn't it propel yourself and your business to move forward and not to repeat the same non-value add activities?

7) Is there anything to stop you and your team from confronting every issue from now on? What do you still fear? Fear of success or failure?

8) Is there any benefit if your team members spin off similar set up of root cause analysis right to their own teams and emulate the same procedures?

11

Kaizen Improvement-
Gemba Kaizen

Gemba Kaizen was endorsed naturally by most, if not all, Japanese corporations immediately after WWII and have thrived successfully with whatever resources that they have left after the war in the region. In modern times many companies have tried and found it difficult to sustain. Kaizen improvement starts from the ground up where the actual issues are inspected and assessed on site. This way of clarification at site is called Gemba Kaizen. Seeing is believing.

There is a Japanese joke that was shared at the opening of a new stone bridge in one of a small Japanese prefecture. During the opening ceremony the authorities engaged a group of blind folks to cross the bridge. The authorities reminded the blind folks that the stone bridge is very strong and there is no need to use their cane to feel their way through. But, as habits die hard, the blind folks continue to use their trusted sticks and feel their way thru the new stone bridge. The moral of the story is: Even after being assured of a condition, you will subconsciously want to check it out with your other senses like gut feel, touch and smell to fill the satisfaction. Gemba Kaizen is exactly that- see, feel, touch and smell at site.

Spending time by keeping still at the place and with a sharp eye for details to spot any variations from the norm is enough to get you going with Gemba Kaizen. Whenever we see an elderly supervisor or Manager in the line trying to solve an issue, they will sit or stand in one particular corner and start to observe and take notes of the variances and non-conformance of certain processes or operations.

By keeping still and spending some reasonable length of time at the same spot will reveal to him the issues that caused the whole process to go haywire. They usually take a longer time to observe and make some concrete assumptions for later confirmation. Once that is settled, the rest is just putting forward some known activities and some unique actions to counter the effect of the problem be it quality, machine defect, materials bottleneck etc.

Not many people have the inclination to do this as it requires some form of identification of variances. The more time these people spend on the line the better the results will be. They are thinking out of the box even though they have been entrenched in this same production line for many years. To assist in this analysis, the total line must have already decided to adopt the best practices of Lean. The work will have to come from the people and the facilitators must firstly be trained and certified by a Kaizen institution so that the teams that he will be leading will be for long term. This is the commitment that the company must make to ensure the success of the Kaizen culture.

Once it is successful in one section, then it can be duplicated to other areas or other affiliated factories whether it is within the same country or abroad. The bigger the commitment given by top management, the bigger the results that contribute to the cost savings as a result of the whole company moving forward in one effort and in one direction. There are no limits to what Gemba Kaizen can do for you as it only can get better and better. It gets repeated all over again until the cost savings are optimized and becomes built into the processes and final products. The beneficiary will be the company and the customers. The customer retention rate will increase and the workers will be loyal to the company. In the 1950s till today, Japanese workers are very loyal to their employers, some worked with the one and only company after they graduated till they officially retired. There are even some retirees who were retained to support the training department to strengthen certain areas of expertise locally and also abroad in affiliated Joint Ventures. Training is needed to sustain what had started as all good things need to revolve continuously as this is what the company's strength is dependent on.

There is no surprise that big corporations allocated at least 5% of their total budget to in-house and external training of key workers and staff. Some have even set up universities for workers who would like to upgrade their knowledge and be a skill certified professional who can apply for a higher position in the same company. Most automotive companies around the world have followed this model as it is very difficult to draw new talents to this field. It also helps to cut short the learning curve of a fresh graduate from another industry to acclimatize to one that is already running at an advanced stage.

Some in-house universities have grown to accept even foreign intakes to take care of the needs of their Joint Venture companies. This is a win-win situation for the company and employee. Communities have also developed around these facilities and factory location and the surrounding towns and villages also prospered. All these are possible because of Lean activities- improving the profitability of the companies and also the livelihood and standard of living of the workers and staff. Nothing has gone to waste and has added value to the whole supply chain network as well running across the country and the whole world.

This gives the whole community and the people who worked in it have a sense of belonging and commitment to look at things as if have the ownership to ensure the smooth running and welfare of the process.

HOW TO ADOPT ATTITUDES OF GEMBA KAIZEN

1) DATA GATHERING: Gemba Kaizen is normally practised at the job site. Imagine yourself like a sponge (a dry one) waiting to mop up a series of liquid stuff. The Gemba approach is something like a Data Grabber- knowing every detail of the issue, the surroundings, the inter-related items and activities, the supporting activities like material handling, surrounding situation and machinery situation. This is what any probe will do- sit still and grab all the information that is needed to analyse the issue and make a good decision to get a good result. Good tips are to be inquisitive and drill down any unclear points until there is clarity (use RCA); test out some assumptions and confirm the effect if something of this sort happens to be involved. For example if the color of the product does not appeal to the customers- then do a quick survey on the colors and confirm whether it is true or not. If it is true, then it's a fact, if not it is just an assumption where no good decisions can be made based on this.

2) VOICE OF CUSTOMER: It is through Gemba Kaizen that the VOC or Voice of Customer surveys have evolved. This is like getting straight answers from the horses' mouth, right from the customers themselves. Similarly during Gemba investigations and assessments, the workers involved will talk-allow them to as there are no holds barred. The truth will set the issues free. The investigation must be impartial and direct. It has to be precise and definite. No grey areas are allowed to prosper and must either be eliminated or parked one side.

3) SETTING PRIORITIES: Priorities are important to allow enough time for confirmation before taking the final action to solve the issue. Use the Pareto Analysis to attacked the Vital Few and leave the Trivial Many as you go along. Eighty percent of the cumulated issues will be addressed firstly and the pareto of the ones most frequently affects the issue will be tackled first. Use the **Pareto Analysis** to prioritise.

Gemba purely requires you and your team to take note of every aspect of the contributors from the 6M covered in the earlier chapter. Run through the contributing factors and list the probable issues by category. Gather existing data to gauge the magnitude of the issues and determine the severity of the issue. The severity can grade each probable factor in accordance to the impact it will have on the process, product or to the customer. The severity of the impact will weigh on the team to address any issue that affects the customer first, then the design and lastly the operations. Usually it is in this sequence of priority. Any issue that affects the customer will be detrimental to the total company. How fast and how responsible your company react to such impact will reflect and gain the customers' trust. We have seen many auto makers announcing recalls that may involve thousands of vehicles that usually have a safety issue with the car and will put the driver and passengers at risk of a fatal accident if the issue is not immediately fixed and contained. This shows the sincerity and commitment of such big corporations that they are always looking out for such issues and correcting them immediately without fear of losing future business. The contrary is true as more customers feel more comfortable for such actions and they will continue to buy future products from such manufacturers.

4) SERIOUS BAD ATTITUDES: Of course the remedial exercise of such issues will incur unexpected expenses of the company and for this reason not very manufacturer will commit themselves to solve such issues immediately. They would rather adopt the 'wait and see' attitude. This is bad and dangerous. In China there was an incident where the baby formula was contaminated with an alternative substance that enhances the protein level in-order to pass certain minimum standard of protein level. What the culprits did (it could be from the unscrupulous milk farm brokers) were they added this substance to enhance the level of protein. It could be an act taken by the brokers to homogenise the milk quality as they have sourced the fresh milk from many milk farms throughout China. They can fool the authorities but the human body cannot be fooled as a few hundred babies died as a result of massive constipation and stomach cramps. Investigators found massive traces of this alternative but harmful substance in the suspected milk formula. All the milk formula were immediately removed from shelves of supermarkets and shops throughout China and also throughout the world. This act of containment prevented further incidences of new cases of sick babies. Eventually, the General Manager of that company who supplied the harmful substance was executed as punishment for murdering the innocent babies.

So, if you think that the right attitude of Gemba Kaizen was introduced in the factory or processing centre of this unscrupulous businessman, do you think such a thing will ever happen?

Obviously not, as Gemba would have caught any of such substances going thru the process. Why did they introduce the additive to enhance the protein level? With Gemba, the team could have isolated each source of the fresh milk and taken readings of the protein levels of each farm. Gemba would have focused on the priority source that contributed to the poor protein level and would have eliminated the poor performing milk farm to boost up the combined lot of milk content.

5) RIGHT ATTITUDES: Gemba Kaizen comes with a full responsibility and commitment and accountability to the impact of the product quality and performance to the customer. This is the attitude that each employee must adopt to ensure the end customer is not in harm's way. Deal with the truth based on actual data. Do not sweep real issues under the carpet as eventually the skeletons in the closets will be revealed as time passed.

Issues are to be solved in a manner that it does not harm the end user or the company be it affecting the health or financial status. The top management must show that in their daily decision making. If the top try to implement some unethical processes then the whole factory will be infested with such unethical practices which will boggle your mind. Things will go wrong but no one is interested to fix it but rather endorse it. It is like a cancer that spreads and will never cease until there is some form of intervention, like a radio-therapy or chemo-therapy to stop the bad cells or bad practices in the case of a company.

The right attitudes must be imbued to every employee and they must swear allegiance to the ideals of the company's Core Ethics and Code of Conduct which permeates trust, integrity and commitment to keep the honor of self and the company.

HOW TO MONITOR AND SUSTAIN GEMBA KAIZEN

1) FOCUSED REVIEWS: Gemba Kaizen focuses on one item at a time before it shifts to another area or issue. There is no need to hurry thru the actions. The diagnostic journey has passed thro the initial Value Stream Mapping, Root Cause Analysis and now Gemba Kaizen. The PDCA cycle is not going to stop here. It keeps revolving and every cycle will need a review of the effectiveness and impact of decisions and actions taken to address the ssues. The way to monitor the progress of the actions are quite simple as it only involves a chart of the key indicators over a period of time. And for every action that is taken, the key indicators are tracked for a period of one month to see the trend. Sometimes, the actions taken do not indicate any progress at all- just remove that particular action and monitor the key indicators again. If it still did not change the status of the issue, then pull it out and implant another action. This is repeated over and over again until there is a change in the result for the better. Most people miss this point about Gemba Kaizen. They easily give up and adopt other more complicated problem solving tools and at times require only the Engineers to do this. But the Engineers do not represent the whole mass of the company. They can solve some issues that are out of the hands of the ordinary workers and technicians which may require months to solve.

2) FULLY ENGAGED: We need the lower level personnel to do their part in a 'down to earth' approach like Gemba Kaizen. Keep it simple and fun and get the people involved on a daily basis. We are not only building culture but we are empowering them to assess and also suggest to management their ideas on how to fix the issues. They are the ones operating the machines or are part of the work process, so they have every right and authority to speak out to make their own jobs easier, fun and accountable for their own actions. Keep them focused on this culture of accountability and we can expect greater things to happen for themselves and the company.

3) TRANSPARENCY: Get the results out in the open to the workers and staff of the company. Be transparent on whether the results are good or bad or whether the actions taken are deemed to be a bit off target. It does not matter because this is what Gemba Kaizen is all about.

Data integrity and the real truth. Unravelling the truth takes time but the results will come quickly if the right decisions and actions take off from there. Develop and publish ready to read visuals at the stations or working cells for the concerned workers to see and read and appreciate their own investigation, actions and results. They will feel good inside that they have achieved something significant or on the contrary feel sad for creating an error or mistake in the process. Admission of guilt is what is missing in most companies these days- putting the blame on others and never to yourself. Stop the blame and deal with the real facts right on- take the bull by the horns and wrestle it down with your team mates until you successfully get off the bull unhurt but jubilant in victory.

4) SHARE TRIUMPHS: Acknowledge great success and publish the triumphs company-wide and also nation-wide if the group has other affiliated companies. It costs nothing to throw an appreciative lunch or dinner to the group that achieved success in conquering the issues. Invite other representatives from other sections that have also tried out Gemba Kaizen techniques to encourage them not to give up but to pursue their goals as well. They need to know that every issue has a light at the end of the dark tunnel as long as they are headed in the right direction and bear in mind it's not an on-coming train.

5) SHARE EXPERIENCES: Send across the leaders from the triumphant group to review and assist and push forward some road blocks in their problem solving process. Motivate them with simpler goals that can be achieved earlier. Stagger and phase out the tasks and goals that seem unachievable within a short time. Break up the ideas and deal with them one at a time and simplify the process so that more people can commit their undivided attention to the issues. Some problems may appear to be like a big elephant. To eat it up you will have to attack the smallest and most vulnerable parts and eventually you will have your stomach's fill. Do not attack hard or difficult areas or else you will have a hard time digesting the issue and end up sick. Remember to take it one step at a time, inch by inch, and you will get to where you wanted to be.

6) COMMUNICATION OF CHANGES: Although the situation has stabilized we know it is still dynamic and all changes to the current state must be duly informed. Generally all Lean Manufacturing facilities or Lean Service providers exercise **CHANGE NOTICES** like:

- Engineering Change Notices, if there are design or process changes
- Quality Standard Change Notices, if certain specifications have been adjusted.
- Personnel Change Notice, if some workers or staff or supervisors are required to change departments or change product lines, then the Safety and Training officer need to know.
- Materials Change Notices, if different vendors have been introduced to ensure incoming inspection is properly executed and differentiated from the next supplier of the same material.

7) CHOICE OF LANGUAGE: It may help if the majority of the workers and staff are English savvy but we may have situations of imported nationals who don't read or write English. You must decide what is the next alternative language needs to be established so that the communication is cascaded correctly without any loss of translation. Dual language is often used to get rid of grey or ambiguous meanings of the original message or content. Precise interpretation and face to face clarification is needed if words cannot describe the real meaning in another language. There are now some well know international signage available in the web or market.

QUESTIONS TO CHALLENGE YOURSELF

1) How would you react to someone of the opposite gender whom you have just met briefly and have written some words of affection towards you? Would you reciprocate the same? Why the procrastination?

2) What if after a few months of courtship the same person wrote the same words to you, would you reciprocate more naturally?

3) You may guess it is more positive as you have grown familiar to the situation and have met the person several times already.

4) Isn't this the same feeling in addressing an issue? Be familiar with the subject at the location where it happened? Don't you have more clarity of the issue to work on it?

5) Have you ever wondered why the problem keep recurring after you have taken some action?

6) Have you ever thought of getting to the location to actually see the problem to appreciate how it came about in the first case?

7) Have your people seen or discover where the contributing factors are coming from that created this issue?

8) Why was it difficult to perform such preliminary actions? Was it because you yourself did not take that first step until it was too late?

12

Other Complementary Problem Solving Tools to Assist Lean

Results are important to gauge the progress of certain actions that have been done to achieve certain objectives. In most cases an action taken based on the analysis of the issues will have to solve that problem that contributed to the issue in the first case. You can be very busy taking action but it may not necessarily solve your problems. However, taking the right actions based on right decisions will definitely give rise to better results.

Let's recall the various steps highlighted in the previous chapters on how to reap the ultimate benefit of implementing Lean:

Step 1: 5S Concepts: Separate the woods from the trees. Implement 5S to remove the clutter in your work and personal life.

Step 2: Value Stream Mapping: Identify the processes that don't add Value to the total Data and Material flow in the manufacturing and service sector.

Step 3: Gemba Kaizen: Seek out the issues at site to have a real feel of the work condition or service related process. It's normally termed as 'feeling the pulse of the situation or issues'

Step 4: Pareto Analysis: State the Issue or Problem (Data gathering and identify the Vital Few and Trivial many contributing factors of the problem). This will prioritise where to address the problem.

Step 5: Fish Bone Analysis: Conduct a brainstorming session to identify and verify the probable Root Causes of the problem.

Step 6: Lean Principles: SLIMWOODS will be reinforced at this stage. The previous steps are the preliminaries needed before Lean can set root and grow.

However, you can implement from whatever step if you have already progressed thru in the past years or months. Don't skip the steps- just build on it till you achieve your goals and targets.

The old saying of "You can only improve what you can measure" rings out very clearly. There are indicators available to measure the effectiveness of Lean implementation:

ON TIME DELIVERY (OTD): This indicator need not be new to you as the customers are your voice of complaints on any untimely deliveries. The OTD measurement have further been modified to include shipments in full quantity and has become known recently as **OTIF (On Time In Full).** Rightfully justifiable as it doesn't count if items are either short shipped or with wrong parts even though they arrived on time, it's as good as not being delivered at all.

How to monitor OTD?: Register all Promised Shipment dates to customers and monitor the number of days the shipment have overshot this date. See the example to calculate the OTD (assuming the goods are received in right quantity and in the right part numbers):

ITEM	1st INDICATION	2nd AGREED DATE
Promised Ship Date in 45 days after receiving Order	1st May	
Actual Delivered Date	21st May	23rd May
Overdue		22 days
% Overdue		100-{(22/(45+22)*100}
% OTD		**67.16%**

What if the goods arrived but are short of some items and of wrong quantity. Usually these parts are quite urgent and are despatched by air freight. And in order to calculate the **OTIF**, the delivery time continues to clock the number of days overdue until the customer confirms receipt of the goods (by air freight).

Then, the calculation of **OTIF** will be calculated as:

ITEM	1st INDICATION	SHORT SHIPMENT
Promised Ship Date in 45 days after receiving Order	1st May	
Short ship Air Freight		30th May
If delivered goods encountered shortage or wrong parts and had to be delivered by air, say to arrive in another 7 days:		
Total Overdue		22+7= 29 days
% Overdue		100-{(29/(45+29)*100}
% OTIF		**65.47%**

From the two measured indicators of this particular shipment, the error contributed by the short shipment is about (67.16 minus 65.47%)= 1.69%

It may appear to be small but to the customer it is a big deal as their succeeding processes are at a standstill and few thousands of lost production and forwarding shipments to their end customers could be in several hundred thousands. Normally, delivery contracts are bound by penalty clauses and this is a good measure to attack the fundamental issues faced during and after shipment to your customers. The **OTIF** is definitely an important KPI for any company that deliver goods.

CYCLE TIME REDUCTION: Cutting wastes in operations will eventually reduce the processing and waiting time. The Cycle Time starts from the first instance a operator retrieves a part from the rack, load it into the machine, wait for machine to process, wait for it to complete and eject, operator retrieves the part and lay into the prepared racks and moves to the parts rack again to retrieve the next loading. The time taken from beginning to the beginning again is termed as the Cycle Time of the process. The contributors that make up the Cycle Time involves the 4Ms (Method, Machine, Man and Materials). It is limited to these key four areas only. Of course there are many more contributors but are quite insignificant. In previous chapters we have already indulged in the various problem solving tools (Pareto Analysis, Root Cause Analysis etc)- use these tools to derive at the root causes of obstacles or lagging activities that appear to clutter the existing value stream. Focus on lean approach and get those waste or non-value add activities out of the way.

How to measure Cycle Time Reduction?: To understand where are the areas to attack for reduction- first of all, the different activities must be measured and compared in a simple time chart:

Process Nbr	Process	Process Time, seconds
1	Move to Material Rack area	50
2	Retreive the material	10
3	Move to Machine area	50
4	Place material into fixtures	20
5	Remove hands from fixtures	8
6	Activate the machine switch	10
7	Machine processes the item	120
8	Machine complete and eject the part	5
9	Remove the items	20
10	Move to racks and place the processes parts	30
11	Move to Material Rack area	50
	Total Cycle time, seconds	373

With a quick glance on the above process- it appears Processes Number 1, 3, 10 and 50 appear to take a longer time as normal. It appears the material rack is placed quite a distance from the place of work. With a Gemba Kaizen team in place (covered in earlier chapters), it should be an easy fix to have the material racks placed closer to the machine.

But, how do we know that the current or new Cycle Time is at the right level? We have touched on TACT time before where we stated that the TACT time is the pulse of production and it's the productive time taken to supply one unit of the total monthly sales units. This is equated to the time needed to produce one unit of the product as demanded by the sales orders for that month. IF the TACT time of the output of the factory is 250 seconds per unit, then all the related

Cycle Time of the processes must be equal to 250 seconds per unit to enable the factory to deliver on time.

For our study, as per the above chart, the Cycle Time of the processes is 373 seconds versus the TACT time of 250 seconds. These is a great opportunity to reduce the Cycle Time to at least 250 seconds so that the process output matches the overall factory TACT time of 250 seconds. For other related processes that are linked in parallel to one another, the individual Cycle time must best be balanced to be in tandem with the TACT time. Usually this is balanced by installing more machines or adding more labour to divide the work content. In most cases lean concepts will take care of non-value add activities.

QUALITY LEVEL UPGRADE: Quality of products coming out of the line is also the area most neglected as it is more complicated and complex to handle by the Quality department. The Quality inspector and Audit section can only gather and analyse the data of defects but they are not the authority to trigger the actions and attach the commitment of the responsible people involved in the process. The workers must be involved in the day to day continuous improvement activities similar to the Kaizen or Quality Control Circles (QCC) to address the issues pertaining to poor quality in a structured manner. The workers know best the real issues and are very resourceful to provide some very smart ideas and proposals for the supporting sections to take quick action to eliminate the issues currently faced by them.

LOST TIME ACCIDENTS: You may think that Lost Time Accidents (LTA) have no relation to Lean but whenever someone gets hurt and could not get back to work after 24 hours of the accident- the lost time has to be filled by someone else. And because of the nature of the job, not anyone can just replace the absent worker. Quality and productivity will be compromised and the products will be held up in one way or another. LTA appear to be ignored if your operations are dependent on non-skilled operators or support staff but there is a social and communal responsibility of the management to ensure personal protective equipment, PPE, are adequately provided to protect the works against, dust, toxic gases and hazardous chemicals etc.

CUSTOMER SATISFACTION INDEX: The CSI is a proactive tool to measure the satisfaction of your customers in relation to the condition of the products or goods delivered. The key parameters measure include packaging, time of delivery, quantity of items, correct items, damages and quick response in the event of encountering major issues. It is quite common for companies to outsource the CSI survey to professionals who will call up the customers once the goods arrive at their premises. The people they will contact will be the supervisors who directly receive the goods and a series of check list will be verified with the person concerned. Any immediate requests will be channeled directly to the supplier's shipping department to take immediate action. At the end of the month all the customers who have received their goods will have given enough data and feedback to the survey company to compile a comprehensive CSI report with ratings from 0 to 10. This data is then utilized by the relevant departments to take appropriate action and also to feedback to the customers directly that the next shipment will not have the same issues.

FLOOR SPACE RECLAIMED: Eventually, when the effects of Lean activities set in, all the layout that have been reorganized for compactness would have freed up free space without you having to put in capital to build another building. The reclamation must be recorded in terms of the square footage saved and calculated based on the present market rate to build a new building or to make an extension for your operations.

NEW PRODUCT LAUNCH TO MARKET: In most big corporations, product launches look easy and have no big fuss in their launches. It usually get executed without any hitches where some companies do rush through their product development to meet tight launch dates resulting in customer complaints on the products etc. In lean management, the new product development would have undergone a thorough check list to ensure nothing is left out in proof-testing the product at every stage of development. Take for example-all Apple smartphone launches are continually done in stages without any hitch and complaints from the expectant customers of its product quality and reliability. The early morning queues at Apple outlets at every new Apple product launch is testimony to the lean approach adopted by Apple.

YOU HAVE ALWAYS WANTED TO READ THIS TYPE OF BOOK

-BUT IS AFRAID TO-

YOU WILL BE AMAZED IF YOU DO

IT UNRAVELS THE SEED OF LEAN PRINCIPLES IN ITS SIMPLIEST FORM

- How did Japan picked itself up from the ruins of the destruction inflicted by two Atomic bombs during WWII- by holding true to the Lean Principles during the toughest of times in their economic history? You can arise too.

- Know why most people and companies find it difficult to implement Lean and its related concepts

- Drop the myth of Lean that it's only created for a certain race or culture and it's not for you and your company

- How Lean thinking have subtly crept into recent innovations and ideas without your knowledge. This book will highlight those incidents or activities

- Lean principles explained in layman's language to present it in a very easy read and comprehension. You will catch the 'Spirit' of Lean as what the original creators were trying to describe it.

- How do we move forward and expect Lean to play a wider role in the near future?

- How do we take Leaner Measures during Tough Times?

Printed in the United States
By Bookmasters